1.⁰⁰

FAIR SHOT

SHOT

RETHINKING INEQUALITY
AND HOW WE EARN

FAIR SHOT

RETHINKING INEQUALITY AND HOW WE EARN

CHRIS HUGHES

St. Martin's Press
New York

FAIR SHOT. Copyright © 2018 by Chris Hughes. All rights reserved.
Printed in the United States of America. For information, address
St. Martin's Press, 175 Fifth Avenue, New York, NY 10010.

www.stmartins.com

The Library of Congress Cataloging-in-Publication
Data is available upon request.

ISBN 978-1-250-19659-0 (hardcover)
ISBN 978-1-250-19661-3 (ebook)

Our books may be purchased in bulk for promotional, educational,
or business use. Please contact your local bookseller or the Macmillan
Corporate and Premium Sales Department at 1-800-221-7945, extension
5442, or by e-mail at MacmillanSpecialMarkets@macmillan.com.

First Edition: February 2018

10 9 8 7 6 5 4 3 2 1

For my parents, Ray and Brenda,
for teaching me that no one is invisible

CONTENTS

FAIR SHOT

RETHINKING INEQUALITY AND HOW WE EARN

INTRODUCTION

In May of 2013, I stood beside a podium on a wooden stage in the center of the Georgia Dome, an indoor stadium in Atlanta. I listened to the president of Georgia State University introduce me to a crowd of 20,000 students and their families attending that year's commencement ceremony. "Chris began his career as an entrepreneur in 2004, when he co-founded Facebook with his Harvard roommates," he said. "In 2007, he became director of online organizing for Barack Obama's campaign." He continued through a few more accolades, and the audience applauded thunderously. I stepped up to the podium to speak to the largest crowd I had ever faced. For a moment, I felt like a rock star.

That moment was brief. In 2012, I bought *The New Republic,* a nearly 100-year-old print magazine, with the intent of stewarding the historic institution and finding a new business model for print media in a digital age. After a string of starry successes, this time my failure was deep, clear, and fast. I overinvested early, set unrealistic goals, and found that I lacked the patience to manage such a difficult transition. By the next year, all of the digital savvy and esteem I had earned was worth nothing to detractors who called me a phony in the pages of *The Washington Post* and *Vanity Fair.*

That was a turning point for me. It confirmed my suspicion that the superficial praise that I had received for years had more to do with what people wanted me to be, rather than who I was. People believed me to be a genius because "Co-Founder of Facebook" followed my name. *Fast Company* once put me on its cover with the headline "The Kid Who Made Obama President," as if I were single-handedly responsible. As soon as the house of cards collapsed, people zeroed in on the power of chance in my story and discounted everything else. I went overnight from a wunderkind to the hapless, lucky roommate of Mark Zuckerberg.

The truth is somewhere in between. For the early part of my life, my story played like a movie reel for the American Dream. I grew up in a middle-class family in a small town in North Carolina. I studied hard, got financial aid to go to a fancy prep school, and then went to Harvard. My roommates and I started Facebook our sophomore year, and my early success there and at the Obama campaign garnered me acclaim and notoriety. Eventually, Facebook's IPO made me a lot of money. I worked my way up, and I took every chance offered to me. I also got very lucky.

That luck wasn't just because I was Mark Zuckerberg's roommate—much larger forces were at work. A collection of economic and political decisions over the past four decades has given rise to unprecedented wealth for a small number of fortunate people, collectively called the one percent. America has created and supported powerful economic forces—specifically globalization, rapid technological development, and the growth of finance—that have made the rise of Larry Page, Jeff Bezos, and other new billionaires possible. The companies we built went from dorm room ideas to assets worth hundreds of billions of dollars because America provided the companies with a fertile environment for explosive growth. Google, Amazon, and Facebook may be extreme examples, but the massive wealth they create for a select few isn't as rare as you might think.

Inequality has now reached levels not seen since 1929, the year the Great Depression began, and stands to get even worse. The same forces that have given rise to massive companies and concentrated wealth have made it more difficult for working people to benefit from the economic opportunity they expect and deserve. By the numbers, Americans are working just as hard as ever but are still struggling to get by. Most Americans cannot find $400 in the case of an emergency like a car accident or a hospitalization, yet I was able to make half a billion dollars for three years of work. Something is profoundly wrong with our economy and in our country, and we have to fix it.

I believe we live at the beginning of a tumultuous era, similar to the turn of the last century, when railroad and shipping tycoons amassed historic fortunes. We need to be as open to creative, new ideas as the most forward-thinking leaders of the Progressive Era were then. They created an income tax, enacted direct elections for senators, banned corporate contributions to political campaigns, enfranchised women, and laid the groundwork for labor protections like the minimum wage and old-age pensions. We need to be equally bold today.

And we should ground our solutions in what works. I have come to believe that, dollar for dollar, the most effective intervention in the fight for economic justice is the simplest: cash, put in the hands of the people who need it most. The guaranteed income is as radical an idea as it is simple. An income floor of $500 per month for every working adult whose family makes less than $50,000 would improve the lives of 90 million Americans and lift 20 million people out of poverty overnight. Wage laborers and informal workers alike—parents with young kids, adults taking care of aging parents, and students—would earn the benefit. It should be paid for by the one percent.

I hope this book starts a broader conversation about why we need a guaranteed income in the United States and how it might work. We can be the generation that ends poverty in America and provides financial stability and economic opportunity to the middle class.

This book traces my journey from a little town in North Carolina to Harvard, through Facebook's blockbuster rise, and to my life afterward. It tells the story of how I grappled with the responsibility of such early "success," and how I came to embrace a guaranteed income. That journey began with poking around blog posts and online forums. It took me to Kenya and back three times and to communities in Ohio, Michigan, North Carolina, California, and Alaska, all in the pursuit of figuring out what works and what doesn't in our economy today.

We have to start having honest conversations about fairness and economic opportunity—even if they are awkward or painful—if we are ever going to fix our country's problems. I hope this book can be a starting point for a frank discussion about the fraying connection between work and wealth, and specifically, how a guaranteed income can restore stability and opportunity to the lives of working Americans.

The American Dream, the idea that we can all do a bit better than the generation that came before us, is an optimistic idea that we should cultivate and reinforce. It has long been more myth than reality, but it is up to all of us, particularly those of us who are benefiting most from the status quo, to work to build a country where everyone has a fair shot to pursue their dreams.

1

HOW
IT
HAPPENS

My father grew up on the grounds of a country club in Mount Airy, North Carolina, the town that inspired Mayberry on *The Andy Griffith Show*. He was born in the early years of the Great Depression, and for the first decade of his life, his parents and he shared a single room in the back of the small clubhouse, heated by a wood stove. His father was the club manager and groundskeeper, and his mother worked in the pro shop. As a kid, he worked as a golf caddy, learning to endear himself to the golfers. When he became a traveling paper salesman as an adult, he used that charm to win the affection and loyalty of his customers.

As he sees it, he picked himself up by his bootstraps and made good on the American Dream, providing our family with a home, a stable income, and a middle-class lifestyle. Today he is 85, and his life's trajectory makes him skeptical that we need a guaranteed income in the United States.

My own life leads me to the opposite conclusion. My success at Facebook taught me that seemingly small events like who you choose to room with in college can have outsized impacts on the rest of your life.

To tell you how my dad and I eventually found common ground, I need to tell you the story of where I grew up, the rocket ship of Facebook's success, and the power of unrestricted cash transfers to transform people's lives.

Our family goes back generations in North Carolina and Virginia, but there is no Southern gentry in our blood.

My mother was part of a large family of rural farmers, Lutherans who emigrated from Germany before the Revolutionary War. They spent the next 200 years tilling the rocky soil in the foothills of Appalachia. Her parents left the farm to become workers in the local textile mill. Both my parents were the first in their families to go to college, and they worked full time in good, stable jobs until they retired. My mom became a public school teacher, and my dad sold industrial paper to small-town printers. They settled down in Hickory, North Carolina, not far from where they grew up. As their respective parents grew older, they picked up the slack and paid many of their bills—they had gone further than anyone in their families ever had, and they were happy to help.

For the first five or six years of my life, our family belonged to New Jerusalem, a small church on the outskirts of Hickory. A simple, redbrick building with a steeple, the church sat on a small hill off a winding two-lane country road. The pastor and his family lived in a little parsonage across the way. The pictures on the stained glass windows inside the nave looked as if they were paint-by-number, and its wooden pews felt like they had been ordered out of a catalog and installed the day before. The cheapness of the setting didn't matter, because the people who came to worship at New Jerusalem knew how to rejoice. Weekly fellowship nights were full of spirited laughter and hugs all around. The latest gossip and group prayers were shared over large bowls of homemade potato salad and plates of fried chicken.

On Sundays after services, congregants milled about on the lawn outside the church's firehouse-red doors and chatted about the hymns they'd sung that day and what was on the menu for Sunday dinner. I loved that hour after church in the sunshine. I remember playing tag with other kids in the maze of legs that surrounded my parents and dashing back to the safety of my mother to hide in the folds of her dress. For a time, my dad served on the church council, and the pastor's wife taught me to read. New Jerusalem felt like a second home.

But it was a long drive there from our actual home in the center of town. A year after I was born, my parents had moved us from a wooden, single-floor ranch-style house in the country into a smaller house in town with a fenced-in backyard just big enough for a little vegetable garden and some grass for our collie-mix, Smokey. The house was cramped even for a family of three, but I had my own room and there was a small sun porch in the back where we made peach ice cream with a hand-cranked machine in the summer. Our home sat a block away from a picture-perfect Southern downtown street lined with mansions that had magnolia trees in their front yards and wisteria vines growing in the back. We lived in the shadow of their grandeur but a world away in spirit.

When I started elementary school, we left New Jerusalem and my parents joined the church a block away from us, Holy Trinity, which happened to be one of the largest and richest in town. Our family walked there every week, my dad and I wearing suits and my mom her Sunday best. Holy Trinity was a fixture of our lives—I can count on one hand the number of Sundays that we didn't attend services—but it was also a place where our family stood out like a sore thumb. It was an enormous and towering building with cold stone floors, and the parishioners were wealthy and wanted you to know it. They liked the elite nature of the church and fought to keep it that way by exercising their snobbery over us. They smiled in the halls but never lingered to chat or invite my parents over for dinner.

I found a couple of friends in Sunday school, but I had a lot less fun with them than I did with the friends I made in the government-run after-school program. Every day after class, I reported to the gym for a couple hours of unstructured homework and play. Almost all of the other kids were black and brown, unlike me, and none of us was rich. Each day, my mom picked me up around five after she had finished teaching and writing her lesson plans.

Our days followed predictable rhythms. My mom made breakfast every morning and dinner every night, and we would go out to eat on Saturdays once a month. We visited my grandparents who lived down the street most evenings and picked up KFC after church to share as an extended family. Weekends were full of chores like mowing the lawn, cleaning the gutters, and vacuuming. My mom clipped coupons from the Sunday paper every week, and we occasionally stopped by the Stouffer's factory to buy rejected frozen meals in bulk for our deep freeze. We were thrifty and cheap, but we always had enough to make ends meet.

My parents worked hard to make sure I got the keys to every room they had been locked out of in their own lives. By the time I was eight, I was invited to join classes for the "gifted"—code in the small-town South for the white and wealthy—and I learned that I could be friends with the after-school kids and the rich kids at the same time. I felt a little like a chameleon, trying to be everything to everyone all at once, pleasing my parents and finding time to be with the friends with whom I was the most relaxed.

As I grew older, I was increasingly socialized into groups of white, wealthy kids, but from early on, I was suspicious of their privilege. I joined sports leagues and enrolled in the manners-building cotillion classes that my parents had never been invited into when they were teenagers. But the rest of the kids in my after-school program, who were just as smart, didn't get tracked into the gifted classes or the cotillion classes or sports teams. Their parents didn't belong to the white church or sit a few pews away from the school principal each Sunday.

While the color of my skin helped me blend in and offered its own set of privileges, it was clear that I was not one of the Hickory elites. We drove an Oldsmobile; the people up the street, Lexuses. We were more devout in our religion, kneeling together as a family each evening for our nightly prayers. The well-to-do went to the country club pool in the summer; we went to the YMCA. I gradually made it into the social class my parents wanted me to be a part of, but in spirit, I knew I never really belonged there. As I became more aware of the world as a teenager, I felt a percolating anger and a desire to defend my parents from the men who snubbed their noses at my dad and the women who never invited my mom to bridge or dinner parties.

By the time I was 14, I had become restless. I was at the top of my class and had a handful of friends, but I found few people who liked the things that I did—classical music, homework, and books. I wasn't clear-eyed about it at the time, but I was gay and in a place where I knew that was anything but okay. My parents told me I could do anything I wanted, and I took their words literally. I wanted to go to a high school where everyone loved to read the fattest books on the shelf and there was a culture of openness and tolerance, unlike the culture of Hickory. One day I searched for "best high school in America" on one of the pre-Google search engines of the early Internet, and I thought I had discovered paradise.

I saw photos of leafy campuses, smiling students, and Oxford-style libraries stacked high with books. Every one of the schools had a gay student group, and a lot of the graduates went to colleges like Yale and Harvard. I applied to several boarding schools, all in liberal New England, without having ever stepped foot anywhere near there. I didn't do it on a lark, but I knew the idea was far-fetched. My parents looked on, unsure if this was part of the plan. I was accepted everywhere I applied. Phillips Academy, often called Andover, offered me a financial aid package, but it wasn't enough. My parents had saved $40,000 to pay for my college, an enormous amount for them, and a single year at Andover cost just shy of that. Even with the financial aid, they would have exhausted the whole $40,000 before I even started college. I called up the admissions agent and explained the situation. They called back and increased the package to nearly a full ride. My parents, nervous and reluctant to see their only child leave so soon, nevertheless agreed to allow me to go.

The day I arrived on campus was idyllic. I had taken a $19 shared SuperShuttle from Boston Logan Airport, and as the blue van pulled up in front of the school, I caught a first glimpse of the vast green lawns, known as the Great Quad, washed in autumn light. Stepping down from the van with a single large rolling suitcase in tow, I must have appeared more than a little out of place. Southern, religious, a scholarship kid, and closeted, I was in a sea of other teenagers with white polo shirts, copper-red shorts, and penny loafers that their parents in finance had bought them over the summer in Nantucket. I had no common language and no common interests with these children of America's elite, who had come from the top private schools and the wealthiest neighborhoods of New York, Los Angeles, Chicago, and Boston. They were friendly enough. No one made fun of me to my face, but neither did they seem all that interested in spending more than a minute or two in my presence.

I settled into a dorm room with a reclusive roommate from Greenwich, a wealthy Connecticut enclave outside New York, and struggled to make friends. Over the following months, I dreaded nothing more than the challenge of finding someone to sit with at meals in one of the school's four dining halls. One was for the popular kids, another for the jocks, a third for theater types, and the fourth for faculty, their kids, and the stray misfit. I tried my hand at each, but every time I sat down with a tray and joined a group, I struggled to know the right thing to say, the right person to be. Afraid of rejection, I froze and ended up saying nothing. I took to skipping meals, filling my stomach with Butterfingers and Reese's from the dorm's basement vending machine instead.

I had made it into the country club, faster than my parents had ever imagined, but that did not mean I fit in. A robust financial aid program had catapulted me to the top of the American social hierarchy nearly overnight, and I was still not "one of them." Instead of trying harder to fit in, I swung hard in the opposite direction, and the rage at anything establishment, authoritarian, or rich that had simmered in Hickory boiled over. I took up smoking—the trashiest kind of cigarettes I could find—and looked for other scholarship kids I could relate to. With few friends and no resources, I fell back on the habits I had brought to the school in the first place and channeled my anger into disciplined study. I wasn't going to embrace the shame of isolation and go home. I intended to beat every single one of those students who'd arrived with first-class educations, designer clothes, and in-born entitlement. I created a community of one in the silent study room of the wood-paneled library.

In time, I started to get the hang of it. Fancying myself an anthropologist in the making, I dropped in on school dances on Saturday nights for an hour or two and hung around the sidelines watching how they worked. I saw how my dorm mates came by each other's rooms casually and made plans to meet one another in the dining hall at a certain time. I began to get the drift. I lost my Southern accent and my religion by the end of my sophomore year. Endless hours of study enabled me to go toe-to-toe with the smartest of the bunch, and I joined the leadership of the campus newspaper and made a real friend. A year later, I made a couple more. In the fall of my senior year, I came out of the closet and got into Harvard with another financial aid package, this time, no haggling required.

The summer after I graduated, I backpacked across Europe on a budget of $20 a day with three friends, studying Botticellis in Rome and how to order coffee properly in France. That fall I arrived at Harvard and realized that I was now one of the immaculately prepared students from a best-in-class school. I still lacked the sense that I belonged, but at least now I knew how to "play the role," as my father had always encouraged me to do. I was only 18 years old that fall, but I knew that friends from Hickory and peers at

Harvard saw in me the kind of "up by the bootstraps" success our country supposedly makes possible.

Then, with the success of Facebook, that story was put on steroids. My sophomore year of college, I chose to room with an acquaintance I had met freshman year, Mark Zuckerberg, in order to be placed in the same dorm as many of my female friends. Dustin Moskovitz and Billy Olson were paired with Mark and me by chance, and the four of us lived in a single suite in Kirkland House. We got along well, but we weren't a tight-knit group. Mark launched multiple projects that fall—a study guide for a class and a now infamous "hot or not" website that compared Harvard students' faces to one another. He was hauled in front of the disciplinary committee for that one.

Around the first of the year in 2004, Mark started talking about a new project that would enable students to voluntarily list themselves on a website. Mark and I had gone to rival boarding schools, Phillips Exeter and Phillips Andover, that were founded by different branches of the same family. Both produced paper "facebooks," spiral-bound directories of their students, printed at the same shop located somewhere between the two. All they contained were the students' names, ID photos, the towns they came from, and their years of enrollment and graduation. As both Mark and I knew, they also provided fodder for endless late-night dorm room conversations: Who was the best-looking? Was this person gay? Would that person make it through the year without getting kicked out? The digital Facebook we launched that winter at Harvard was not specifically built to imitate those spiral-bound relics from high school, but it felt similar because it tapped into the same desire to gaze at others and collectively judge. Most importantly, unlike the paper books where you had no control over how you looked, Facebook gave you the power to choose which profile photo was just right—at least for the self you wanted to be for the next hour or two. That's how the obsession with Facebook took root in the early days: you had to constantly click around to see who had updated their profiles most recently, sleuth out what they had changed, and speculate as to why.

The initial version of Facebook we launched was bare-bones, similar to the popular open social network Friendster, but open only to Harvard students. Mark was user number four, I was number five, and our roommate Dustin was number six. (Users one through three were test accounts.) We sent a few e-mails to our friends inviting them to join, and within three weeks, 6,000 students signed up. The rocket ship began to take off.

While Mark enlisted Dustin to help build the site and open it up to other colleges, I prepared promotional plans for Harvard and the new schools and helped design core features on the site, like messaging and an early news product. The non-techie of the group, I took responsibility for how the site might be used and how others might perceive it. I pitched in wherever I could to tweak a feature, improve an interface, or make sure a reporter knew the facts. At that stage, Facebook was mostly a fun side project, more something to bond with my roommates over than a way to change the world. Seeing how quickly we could make it grow was almost like a game.

Mark, however, talked about Facebook in near-religious terms from the outset: he saw it as a way to make the whole world more "open and connected." When reporters described it as a social network for college kids, he chafed at how little they appreciated the scope of his ambition. He exhibited the raw confidence of a natural leader who strikes out on a new path and inspires others to follow, and I joined the army. A few months after the launch, our posse had grown to nearly a dozen, and that summer, we landed in a house in Palo Alto on La Jennifer Way.

Mark and Dustin decided not to return to Harvard that fall, but the idea of dropping out held little allure for me. On scholarship and with no financial cushion or family money to fall back on, I was still in awe that I had made it to a place like Harvard in the first place. My junior year I fit work on Facebook into the rest of my studies, but the time it required grew significantly as the months passed. I returned to Palo Alto the next summer, and eventually commuted back and forth every few weeks during my senior year. After graduating, I joined the company full time, ready to see where it might lead.

As Facebook grew, the area I ran officially became the department of communications and marketing. There were press releases to write, proactive communications and marketing campaigns to plan, and public relations crises to handle. When I joined the crew full time in the summer of 2006, I moved to the product team and worked with engineers to develop new features and upgrade what users saw and did on the site. In less than a year, we launched the running homepage called News Feed that still anchors the site, opened the platform to non-college users, and integrated the first sharing functionality that made it possible for people to exchange, post, and comment on links inside the site. We moved fast and broke things, the classic Facebook maxim that was plastered to the walls in Facebook's headquarters.

Every day, it seemed, we passed a new milestone. We hit a record number of users nearly every week, and investors responded by pouring more money in. We had such momentum that I failed to notice how often the goalposts kept moving further out. We hadn't expected it to catch on like wildfire in a matter of days at Harvard, and it seemed insane when a venture capital firm valued the company at an eye-popping $100 million only a year later. Yahoo offered us $1 billion to buy the company a year after that. We were 22 years old, but we passed on the offer.

To my friends at home who were just as addicted to Facebook as everyone else, I was a hero. To my parents, I had become everything they had hoped for—a small-town kid who had made it big. Even before Facebook's public offering and the wealth that came with it, I felt a sense of pride that I had channeled the restless energy of my teenage years into the opportunity to go to great schools and build a fruitful career, albeit more quickly than I'd imagined. I knew that I had worked hard in school and later on Facebook, and I was proud of the savvy I'd shown in the projects I'd chosen to become involved in. Despite my lack of engineering skills, I had found a way to make myself valuable to the company as it grew.

In the years after Facebook's success, the story of its founding and rise became one of the great legends of entrepreneurial America. (Aaron Sorkin's 2010 film *The Social Network* only added fuel to the fire.) Long after I left the company, civic groups, companies, and schools invited me to visit and tell the story of Facebook in a way that would inspire and galvanize. Listeners were anxious to believe that their own smarts and elbow grease could earn them similar success; they wanted to know the secret of how we did it so that they might be next. I struggled to give these crowds what they wanted. I knew what it felt like to achieve great things after working hard for them, and Facebook was indeed an incredible success story. But it was a starkly different kind of success than any of my ancestors had lived. Each generation had worked hard and done a little better than the one that came before. But what we'd experienced at Facebook felt more like winning the lottery.

Everyone else was enthralled by the picture of a dorm room success story, but I was unconvinced. I didn't feel like some kind of genius, and while Mark was smart and talented, so were many of the other people I went to college with. Close confidants wondered if I suffered from the "impostor syndrome" that psychologists talk about, in which successful people can't accept or acknowledge their own accomplishments. I didn't think so. It wasn't a lack of confidence that kept my ego in check, but a sense that unique circumstances had more to do with our success than others realized.

As I grew older, left Facebook, and became wealthy after its public offering, I began to look around at other similarly "successful" rich people, the kind of kids I had gone to Harvard with and other young entrepreneurs who had made money quickly in Palo Alto. I began to question how much they "deserved" their success and what role forces outside their control had played. Was my experience at Facebook unique, or was it just one example of something much bigger going on in our country?

2

THE DISMANTLING OF THE AMERICAN DREAM

The rain beat steadily on the wooden roof of John Hicks House, a tiny eighteenth-century home in Cambridge, Massachusetts, that had been converted into one of Harvard's libraries. I was working there in a $10-an-hour job where I sat by the entrance and theoretically checked IDs as students came in. I should have been finishing a paper that was due the next day, but instead I was chatting on AOL Instant Messenger, Mark's preferred method of communication for serious conversations, and the talk we had been having for the past hour was getting serious. "My shift is ending," I typed. "I'll come by the room."

"I have to go to the science center," Mark wrote back. "Up for a walk?" I closed my laptop and headed out into the rain.

Mark and I had been spending a lot of time together. We had released Facebook a month or two before, and it had exploded in popularity. Mark was struggling to keep the site up and running for the unexpected flood of users, while furiously coding for an imminent expansion to Yale, Stanford, and other schools. As if that wasn't enough, at the same time he was tutoring our third roommate, Dustin, on the fundamentals of computer programming so he could pitch in. A photo from that period that ran in Harvard's newspaper, *The Crimson,* shows Mark at his desk, a half-dozen empty soda bottles at his side, his hair overgrown but freshly combed. I remember the scramble to make him look civilized for the shot, and we were barely successful.

I had spent the frantic weeks since the launch preparing for moments like that, developing a communications plan to explain what Facebook was and what we wanted it to be, answering phone calls from the local press, and laying the groundwork for the expansion to new schools. We wanted students at the next colleges to become as obsessed as Harvard students were with which profile photo to choose (users could only have one) and how to curate the perfect list of "Favorite Movies."

What Mark and I had been messaging about that night was my ownership stake in Facebook, now that it was becoming a real business. We met under the portico of our dorm and headed out into the rain. I had a single umbrella for both of us. "I want 10 percent," I said as we walked. I wasn't sure if he heard me the first time—the rain pounded onto the umbrella I was awkwardly holding over the two of us—so I said it again, but it came out sounding more like a demand. "I want 10 percent!" The number felt a little ambitious, but not entirely unreasonable. I had brushed up on the rudiments of effective bargaining and decided to start high.

"I just don't think you've earned that much," Mark answered. I paused and took a little time to respond, thinking to myself, *This might matter someday.* "I appreciate what you are doing," Mark continued, "and I think you could do a lot more as we grow the site, but I need to keep control. And the others need fair equity too."

The rain turned into a downpour, and our steps quickened. This was the worst way to have such an important conversation, but our suite wouldn't have been much better. Mark and I shared a cramped bedroom that barely fit our two twin beds. Dustin shared a similarly small bedroom with our fourth roommate Billy, who had chosen not to participate in anything Facebook-related. Our common room had just enough space for our four desks and a small futon. There was little room for in-person, private conversations, let alone a business conversation that might turn into an argument.

I am conflict-averse by nature, and I found myself in this moment, one of the most important of my life, unprepared and of two minds myself. I felt I deserved a piece of the rapidly growing pie, but I recognized I was a less critical member of the team than Mark or Dustin. The idea for the network had been entirely Mark's, and Dustin was sleeping three or four hours a night to fit in schoolwork, lessons on how to code, and early engineering work for the site itself. I was actively engaged as our storyteller—Mark dubbed me the "Empath" on the first version of our "About" page—but my role was secondary and I knew it. I wasn't in a position to make demands, but I was anxious to become more involved. Facebook felt different to me than the other quick-build websites Mark had launched, and I was increasingly excited to be a part of something that could be big, culturally and commercially, at Harvard and beyond.

As Mark and I walked up Holyoke Street and entered Harvard Yard, I argued that carefully communicating the story of Facebook was critical to its virality and to securing our users' trust. "People are signing up because the site is good, and it's good because they know us and they know they can trust it," I said. "We are not an anonymous Internet company—we are their peers." Mark agreed, but he didn't move any closer to my number.

By the steps of Widener Library in the center of Harvard Yard, I caved. "Just give me what you think is fair. I know it's hard to balance all of us." Frustrated, tired, and late to whatever meeting he was going to, Mark replied with a simple "Okay" and walked off—no umbrella, no hoodie—directly into the pouring rain. A few weeks later I found out that Mark had given me around 2 percent of equity in the company, and that Dustin had gotten several times more. Mark, of course, had retained control for himself. We didn't know it at the time, but we were children on the precipice of becoming richer than royalty.

A few seemingly small decisions, like that conversation in the rain for me, altered the trajectories of our entire lives. Facebook was reincorporated a few months later, decreasing my percentage slightly, and my share gradually shrank as the company raised hundreds of millions of dollars over the coming years. I did not know to exercise my stock options in the early days, so I had to wait until the public offering, a simple error that resulted in a tax bill several times higher than normal for start-up founders. (I had no tax advisors, investment managers, or wealthy family to give me pointers on how to be "tax efficient.") But for all my weak negotiating skills, poor financial decisions, and modest role in the enterprise, I walked away with nearly half a billion dollars.

Over the next decade, Facebook grew precipitously. After capturing nearly the entirety of the college market and making inroads into high schools, we opened our doors to the whole world in the fall of 2006. Our goal became to create a web of human connection, the pipes people could use to share thoughts and feelings with friends and family around the world. The ambition of the vision—"to make the world more open and connected"—inspired users, employees, and investors alike. By the time Facebook went public eight years after our launch, it had raised over $600 million in venture capital and nearly a billion people used the platform. Today, 2 billion people—two-thirds of all people on the Internet—actively use Facebook, and the company is valued at $500 billion. This kind of growth is extreme, but it is not altogether unusual for a tech company in the era that we live in.

The seeds of Facebook's success were not planted in 2004 at its founding, but in the late 1970s, before any of us had even been born. In that decade America's political leaders began to lay the groundwork for the economic forces that made Facebook possible. They're the same forces that compel us to create a guaranteed income today.

In the decades following the Great Depression, the size and power of government consistently grew, even under Republican presidents like Richard Nixon. Government was largely perceived to be a trusted force for good, a powerful institution increasingly able to guarantee civil rights and provide critical social services like broader access to education and health care. While Nixon's record on social issues like crime and race mean that we remember him as a serious conservative, he energetically competed for the political center on economic issues, overseeing the biggest increase in domestic spending in decades. He created new government agencies to protect the environment and to expand workplace safety. When he resigned in disgrace over the Watergate scandal, government spending as a percentage of GDP was at an all-time high, more than it had been even during the fiscal stimulus of the Great Depression.

As government expanded, even under a Republican president, corporations felt their interests increasingly marginalized. After several years of new regulations and more taxes, businesses began to self-organize in the mid-1970s to fight back against the Washington elites who they believed were neglecting their interests. Wealthy companies across industries coordinated to create the largest lobbying effort ever seen in the United States, which eventually became a permanent fixture in our politics. Just under 200 firms had registered lobbyists in 1971, but a decade later, nearly 2,500 did. Meanwhile, corporate political action committees, known as PACs, increased their expenditures in congressional races fivefold in just a decade. Alongside these new PACs and lobbying outfits, businesses transformed small, sleepy think tanks like the American Enterprise Institute and the Heritage Foundation into ideological juggernauts to provide an intellectual justification for a new brand of conservatism that could go toe-to-toe with the domestic liberal consensus of the time.

These new organizations helped to fundamentally shift the nature of our economy. Right off the bat, they managed to kill the creation of a new consumer advocacy organization, the banner proposal of Jimmy Carter's first year as president. A year later, they blocked new labor protections and cut taxes on the investment income of the wealthy, while increasing payroll tax rates that ordinary working Americans pay. They were just getting warmed up. Over the following decades, Ronald Reagan and George H. W. Bush's administrations oversaw the deregulation of major industries, reductions in tariffs that allowed for rapid increases in globalized trade, and deep tax cuts that disproportionately benefited the wealthy. The top tax rate of 75 percent in 1968 dropped to 28 percent by 1988. In the midst of deregulation and the across-the-board reduction in taxes, the one place they did invest was in the Department of Defense.

All these changes laid the groundwork for three forces—rapid advances in new technologies, globalized trade, and the rise of finance and venture capital—that made Facebook possible.

It's obvious Facebook wouldn't exist without the Internet, but few people know that the Internet itself was the direct result of government-funded research. A major beneficiary of the increase in defense spending was ARPANET, which established the early protocols that enabled computers to speak to one another. The National Science Foundation later invested to create national supercomputing centers at major colleges and universities, and the early Internet connected them to one another by 1986. Within a few years, commercial Internet service providers emerged, and people began to use the World Wide Web, the usable interface for today's Internet.

The Wild West structure of the early Internet enabled a few companies to corner very large markets. The early web was flat and open: no global authority regulated the Internet, outside of how the address system worked. Web users could move about anonymously, and the lack of regulatory structure made for a kind of chaotic freedom. One voice on early message boards was just as loud as any other, and someone with a good idea and a small bit of tech savvy, like us in our college dorm room, could throw up a website and access millions of people willing to try out anything new.

But the openness also allowed early entrants to enjoy first-mover advantages that latecomers could not recapture. Just like in any land rush, whether in nineteenth-century America or the economy in post-Soviet Russia, after a brief period of seemingly egalitarian chaos, a few major players consolidated power. Four companies now control the vast majority of our interactions on the web. The real land rush on the Internet did not happen in the late 1990s when early users began to trickle in, but a decade later in the 2000s, the exact moment when we started Facebook.

When Mark coded the first lines in the early days of 2004, only a third of people in the developed world were using the Internet at all. Today over 80 percent are, and Facebook was perfectly poised to capture nearly all of them. Like Google and Amazon, which had a few years' head start on us, Facebook began operations in this sweet-spot period in history when the size of the web was modest and quickly growing. The largest firm founded since Facebook is Uber, valued at only a tenth of Facebook's size. We started Facebook just in time to ride the wave of the web's explosive growth.

The lowering of tariffs and the embrace of a globalized market was the second force behind Facebook's rise. Because Washington had relaxed trade rules decades before, it became possible for companies to manufacture smartphones cheaply, driving a dramatic increase in Internet users. Millions of people who couldn't afford a home computer came online with iPhones and similar devices. Businesspeople had been using smartphones for years, but as the phones became more affordable and popular, the amount of time mobile users spent on Facebook surged quickly past the time spent on computers. There are over 2 billion smartphone users in the world today, and for most people, it's the primary way they access the Internet and use Facebook.

The early growth of the iPhone—the first mass smartphone—is entirely a result of this global market. Apple strategically used the lack of tariffs and cheaper and more efficient transportation networks to build an expansive network of suppliers across the globe. To build an iPhone, the company sources precious minerals from the Congo and touch-screen glass from Taiwan, imports camera lenses from Japan and circuit boards from Malaysia. It buys accelerometers from Germany and optical sensors from Austria. The company assembles all of these parts with labor in China and designs the devices from its headquarters in California. The price of the introductory model today runs $14 a month with a two-year contract, making it affordable for almost all Americans.

The explosion of mobile has been the biggest and most important event in Facebook's success, but at first, it didn't seem like a sure bet. I remember an early set of conversations between Dustin and Mark in 2007, when Dustin pushed Mark to prepare faster for the tsunami of mobile users just around the bend. Mark was skeptical, and Dustin couldn't manage to convince him. Dustin's prediction was a little early, but Facebook was indeed caught flat-footed when the surge in mobile users arrived in 2011. As late as that year, Facebook had only a handful of engineers focused on its mobile products, but it immediately pivoted to capture the emerging market, yielding enormous returns. Facebook went from zero mobile advertising revenue at the time of its initial public offering in 2012 to $22 billion a year by 2016. This kind of hockey stick revenue growth is indicative of what happens when a company has already cornered a market so clearly that nearly all it has to do is flip a switch and the money comes pouring in. Facebook had already locked virtually every Internet user into its walled garden, giving them a massive edge to take advantage of the mobile market when it emerged.

Facebook today works almost like the telephone lines of the past, particularly when you take into account its messaging services. The average user spends nearly an hour a day on the platform, more time than most people spend reading or exercising, and nearly as much time as the average person spends eating and drinking. This does not include the time spent on WhatsApp, the world's largest messaging platform, or Instagram, the world's largest photo sharing app, both owned by Facebook. Billions of people rely on Facebook's backbone to stay in touch, the culmination of Mark's early ambition to create a "social utility" to wire the world. It is the primary means for new parents to announce the births of their children and the first place we go in the case of a natural disaster to make sure our loved ones are okay. All told, nearly 80 percent of all the world's social traffic is routed through Facebook's servers.

But even with all of these unprecedented opportunities, a third force fueled Facebook's rise: the massive amount of financial capital made available to us by venture capitalists. A historically unprecedented run-up in the markets—combined with historic lows in tax rates—put large amounts of capital in the hands of high-net-worth individuals, pension funds, and university endowments in the 1980s and 1990s. Venture capital firms in particular promised high-net-worth individuals and institutions eye-popping returns from high-risk, low-tax investments, for a not-so-small fee. Venture capitalists plan for seven out of ten of their investments to fail, two to break even, and one to explode in value, wiping out all of the other losses and guaranteeing a high return. That's the theory; in reality, in the past 15 years, most venture capital firms have not posted much better returns than the public markets. Investors poured tens of billions of dollars into venture firms in the late 1990s and early 2000s, and that money was invested in companies like Facebook. (They're still going—venture capitalists and independent early stage investors invested $80 billion in new companies last year alone.) There is no historical precedent for this amount of capital being invested in risky early stage ideas.

To my inexperienced eyes, the amount of money invested in Facebook in the early years was jaw-dropping. In the spring of 2005, I visited the offices of Accel Partners on University Avenue in downtown Palo Alto. At Facebook, we were crammed into a smelly office sublet a few blocks away, but here, everything was calm and clean. Pristine marble and orchids lined the library-quiet space. I marveled that the little website we were running from our dumpy office moved these kinds of people to invest over $12 million, only a year after we started the company. That investment decision changed my life personally, and the lives of the other co-founders. Mark, Dustin, and our then president Sean Parker pocketed a million each from that one investment round, regardless of whether Facebook succeeded or flopped. I got $100,000, a windfall that gave me basic security unlike anything I had ever experienced. A year later, all of us were finally 21 years old, and we could celebrate with champagne when other firms invested another $28 million in the company. In total, financial firms invested over $600 million in Facebook while it was still private.

Because of outdated SEC regulations, most companies prefer to wait as long as possible to go public to avoid the regulations and public oversight that come with being traded on public markets. The effect of these policies is that no average American has any way to buy shares in the early days of the lives of valuable companies, but the networked ultra-wealthy are able to get a slice of them through these firms. In Facebook's case, they were handsomely rewarded.

The growth of venture capital is a small piece in a much larger story of the rise of finance over the past few decades. As more money pools in the bank accounts of the rich, private equity firms, venture capital groups, and hedge funds have more capital to invest. The effect of this gargantuan financial sector is that nearly limitless capital is available to young entrepreneurs, regardless of their long-term performance, and less money in the pockets of working people, as we will see.

Facebook would not exist, at least in the form it is today, without major advances in technology, globalized markets that made smartphones possible, or venture capital. Alan Krueger, the former chair of the Council of Economic Advisers and an award-winning economist at Princeton, uses the term "winner-take-all" economy to describe the state we live in today. "Over recent decades, technological change, globalization and an erosion of the institutions and practices that support shared prosperity in the U.S. have put the middle class under increasing stress," Krueger argued in a 2013 speech. "The lucky and the talented—and it is often hard to tell the difference—have been doing better and better, while the vast majority has struggled to keep up." The term *winner-take-all,* first used to describe today's economy by Robert Frank and Philip Cook in the 1990s, is purposefully broad, a way to characterize the effects of a collection of diverse economic forces, including automation and globalization.

In a winner-take-all world, a small group of people get outsized returns as a result of early actions they take. These small differences that later yield big successes are often called luck, but luck isn't really the right word. It implies that no work happens or that success is completely untied from effort. Mega-successes are almost always the result of a blend of fortune and effort. J. K. Rowling, the first billionaire author in history, had her Harry Potter novel rejected by twelve publishers, before a thirteenth gave it a shot. Her success was earned—her persistence paid off—*and* was the result of a small decision by the thirteenth publisher that changed her life. In my case, the chance that Mark Zuckerberg and I ended up roommates changed my life. I had worked hard to get to Harvard, and I played a meaningful role in the early days of Facebook. But the combination of those small events led to outsized and historically unprecedented returns thanks to the magnifying power of today's economic forces.

Michael Lewis, now one of the best-selling nonfiction authors in the world, similarly benefited from a blend of fortune and hard work. A couple of years after he graduated college, he was coincidentally seated next to the wife of a Salomon Brothers executive at a dinner party. As Lewis tells the story, the woman, won over by his charm, convinced her husband to offer him a job trading derivatives, at the exact moment that those complex and risky new products were beginning to transform Wall Street beyond recognition.

He spent three years trading, making quite a bit of money, and then, at age 28, published *Liar's Poker,* his account of the turbulent epoch he had just lived through and witnessed firsthand. It was a massive hit, and it brought him a tidal wave of attention. In 2012, he gave the commencement address at his alma mater, Princeton, on the topic of his luck:

> All of a sudden people were telling me I was born to be a writer. This was absurd. Even I could see there was another, truer narrative, with luck as its theme. What were the odds of being seated at that dinner next to that Salomon Brothers lady? Of landing inside the best Wall Street

firm from which to write the story of an age? Of landing in the seat with the best view of the business? Of having parents who didn't disinherit me but instead sighed and said "do it if you must"? Of having had that sense of must kindled inside me by a professor of art history at Princeton? Of having been let into Princeton in the first place?

Saying people get lucky is not a denial that they work hard and deserve positive outcomes. It is a way of acknowledging that in a winner-take-all economy, small, chance encounters—like who you sit next to at a dinner party or who your college roommate is—have a more significant impact than they have ever had before. In some cases, the collections of these small differences can add up to create immense fortunes.

Last spring, Mark Zuckerberg returned to our old stomping grounds to give a commencement speech of his own. He spoke a stone's throw away from where we had negotiated ownership stakes in Facebook thirteen years before. In his speech Mark wondered whether the hard-working young graduates before him sufficiently appreciated the role that chance and good fortune have already played in their lives. "We all know we don't succeed just by having a good idea or working hard. We succeed by being lucky too," he said from the august lectern. "If I had to support my family growing up instead of having time to code, if I didn't know I'd be fine if Facebook didn't work out, I wouldn't be standing here today. If we're honest, we all know how much luck we've had."

But luck doesn't just happen. We have created an economy dominated by forces that reward luck in an outsized way. Some of these changes might be desirable and some not, but they are all the result of political decisions that we purposefully make as a society. There is no invisible hand creating a winner-take-all economy in which luck takes on this disproportionate role. We are its authors and enablers.

The natural result of our collective decision-making over the past decades is an economy in which a small number of people hit the jackpot each year. I'm not talking about the local dentist, lawyer, or doctor, the kind of rich folks I grew up around in North Carolina. I am talking about the families in households of the top one percent by income or wealth. Families that have more than $10 million in assets. By contrast, the average doctor in my hometown last year made $189,000, and like most wealthy Americans, was assuredly not part of the one percent. The people I'm talking about are people like me and my neighbors in Manhattan. They are CEOs at S&P 500 companies who, on average, are paid 347 times more than the typical worker at their company, a remarkable increase from the historical average of 20 to 60 times. They are superstar athletes, real estate agents and developers, and blockbuster lawyers, the most elite in each of their fields. They are also overwhelmingly not diverse: 96 percent of the ultra-wealthy one percent are white.

The result is an unprecedented collection of wealth controlled by a small number of families. A single family, the Waltons, all of whom inherited their wealth from the Walmart empire, now controls as much wealth as the bottom 43 percent of the country combined—137 million Americans. Just the top 0.1 percent of our population—the 160,000 or so families who have $20 million or more—control the same amount as the entire bottom 90 percent of Americans combined. The chasm between the rich and the poor has not been so wide since 1929, the year of the biggest collapse in Wall Street's history.

The problem isn't that our new economy has fueled the rise of Facebook and mega-winners. It's that the growth of the ultra-wealthy has come at the expense of everyday Americans. Rapid technological advances, globalization, and financialization are pulling the rug out from under the middle class and lower-income Americans. The same forces that enabled the rise of Facebook, Google, and Amazon have undermined the stability and economic opportunity that most Americans have a right to expect.

Of all of the effects that these economic forces have unleashed, the most pronounced is the destruction of full-time jobs and the rise of contract labor, often symbolized by the Uber drivers of the "gig economy." Ironically, technology has taken us backward and made jobs look more like what they were for most of our country's history: poorly paid and precarious. We tend to think that the gig economy is a new phenomenon, but the mid-twentieth century was a brief interlude in a long history in which jobs were more often than not unreliable.

Before the second half of the twentieth century, work was more likely to be at home on the farm or in a short-term stint somewhere, in the kinds of jobs my grandfather had as a young man. He grew up in a small house that sat on a few acres of rocky land in northwestern North Carolina, a mile from the Virginia border. The sixth of seven children, he quit school when he was 15 to help his family grow vegetables, raise chickens, milk cows, and generally keep the family farm in order. His first experience of a "job" was close to home, seasonally dependent, and tied to the completion of small, discrete tasks. His parents paid him with food and shelter.

With historically bad timing, his parents decided to uproot the whole Hughes clan, including my grandfather's new wife, Thelma, and move to Philadelphia to take advantage of the economic boom of the roaring 1920s. They arrived in 1929, just in time for the stock market's collapse. For the next two years, my grandparents lived alongside 11 other people in a standalone house in Philadelphia's Frankford neighborhood. Lacking any education or nonfarm skills, my grandfather decided that he would become a barber. In my imagination, I see a Southern kid roaming about a dense Philadelphia neighborhood waiting for a client in need, like a Lyft or Uber driver of today except with a pair of scissors in hand.

My grandfather *had* cut hair—he had those shears to prove it—but he had never really been a barber like the barbers

I would later see as an adult. (The bowl cuts he gave me as a kid confirmed that he had failed to develop any meaningful skill.) Crammed in like sardines with his family in a new city, he learned to make do because anything that contributed to the family's income, even a few dollars, helped.

It wasn't just my grandfather whose life reflected the precarious nature of work at the time. In the 1930 census, only three out of the nine working-age people in my grandparents' crowded Philadelphia household had ever earned a steady income from a full-time job. My grandfather's brother-in-law had been a molder in the furniture industry, his brother had been a hide sorter in a tannery, and his sister was a stenographer at an insurance company. Everyone else picked up whatever gig they could find.

But then my grandfather's economic prospects brightened, mirroring what happened to many in the rest of the country. He landed the job of country club manager and groundskeeper back home in North Carolina, which required a lot more than 40 hours a week of work but provided housing and relative stability. He was paid $30 a month (roughly $430 a month or $5,000 a year in today's dollars), plus free board. My grandmother came as part of the "package deal" and became the sole person staffing the pro shop and food stand. These jobs brought them much-needed independence from their extended families and some stability, but it was still far from a living wage for a young family of three.

The economic growth that lifted many Americans up over the following decades did the same for my family.

When my grandfather served in the Second World War, my grandmother worked in a local diner, as many hours a week as she could get. After the war, she found stable employment as a worker in a hosiery mill and worked the next 30 years as a manager overseeing the looms that made socks and hose. In the 1950s, my grandfather became a medium-haul truck driver for an oil company, and while his schedule remained irregular, his paycheck arrived every two weeks, a heartbeat of stability in the background of their lives.

My parents got their first jobs in the 1950s and 1960s. They not only enjoyed the security of regular paychecks, but also had the added benefits of employer-provided health insurance, paid sick days, vacation time, and pensions.

For the three decades spanning 1950 to 1980, most Americans, particularly white men, were able to find steady work in jobs that provided the foundation for a stable, middle-class life. Companies provided a suite of wraparound services that guaranteed stability in their employees' lives. In 1955, a big corporation like Kodak spent $1,000 per year, roughly $8,000 today, on life insurance, retirement, sick pay, disability benefits, and vacation pay for each employee. Employees with 15 years of service or more received medical care for life, not just for themselves, but also for their dependents. This period of stable jobs and nearly full employment was a brief historical exception, but it has been burnished in our collective psyches as a golden age.

The short period came to an end as globalization, rapid technological advancements, and the rise of finance modified the nature of jobs so that they became more precarious and piecemeal. If my parents were ten years younger, my father likely would have lost his paper-selling job and been out of work, thanks to the collapse of small-town printers in the digital transition and the rapid consolidation in the industry powered by finance. He would almost certainly now be looking for a new career—or some task to get paid for— very late in life. My mother would be making less money than she did decades earlier because wages for teachers in North Carolina have not kept up with inflation, let alone today's higher cost of living. They, like most Americans, especially those working for private sector businesses, would be falling behind at a moment in their lives when they need security more than ever. "For workers, the American corporation used to act as a shock absorber. Now, it's a roller coaster," the journalist Rick Wartzman writes.

When unemployed people in urban areas find themselves without jobs or marketable skills today, they do what my grandfather did. Instead of reaching for a pair of barber shears, they reach for their smartphones and register to become Lyft drivers and Postmates delivery people. Task Rabbiters pitch in to assemble furniture, rake leaves, or even stand in line to buy theater tickets or a newly released iPhone. In some cases, these contract jobs are a godsend because they help workers who only get part-time hours elsewhere to supplement their income, as laborers have done since the beginning of time. We often think of millennials in these jobs, the masters of the art of the "side hustle," but the numbers show it isn't just millennials doing contingent work. A quarter of the working-age population in the United States and Europe engage in some type of independently paid gig, some by choice, but many out of necessity.

People who find work through apps like Lyft and Task-Rabbit get a lot of attention, but they are the tip of the iceberg. The instability that characterizes their work has spread throughout the economy as the class of low-quality jobs has grown. If you include not only independent gigs, but part-time workers, temps, and on-call workers, the number of people working in contingent jobs balloons to over 40 percent of all American workers. The blue collar jobs of yesteryear that paid decent salaries and provided benefits have declined from about half of overall jobs 60 years ago to around 20 percent today. A Princeton study found that of all the jobs created between 2005 and 2015, 94 percent of them were contract or temporary, meaning virtually every job we created in the last decade was piecemeal and the income was unreliable.

Many of these jobs of the new economy pay poorly, require flexible schedules, and do not offer the stability of benefits or guaranteed pay. People in these jobs are Starbucks and Walmart employees who barely get 20 hours of work a week, babysitters and dog walkers, consultants and delivery people. Some of these workers may get to choose when they work, but they are more often beholden to when the market is ready to employ their services. Some days they may have a boatload of customers, and others, none. (Even when they do have a lot of customers, Uber drivers make barely $15 an hour before accounting for expenses like gas, maintenance, or depreciation of their cars.) Contract and part-time workers may be able to make some money, but they don't have any of the stability or the opportunity to get ahead that a traditional job brought in the middle of the twentieth century.

As contract work has expanded, wages for traditional, full-time jobs have stagnated. In May 2017, I stood on the front porch of a home in Warren, Ohio, and chatted through a screen door with a woman I will call Julie, while her daughter watched television behind her. I had come to northeast Ohio at the invitation of the Ohio Organizing Collaborative, a coalition of community organizations, faith institutions, labor unions, and policy groups, to talk with people affected by the forces that gave rise to Facebook. Julie lived in a white, traditionally Democratic neighborhood that had voted for Donald Trump. Across from her house was a deserted, half-demolished parking lot, and behind it loomed an abandoned factory. Julie seemed calm and resilient, but she was visibly exhausted. She had a job as an office manager at the local school, and her husband worked nights in a pipe factory. All around them property values were in a free fall, and there was little hope on the horizon. "We are treading water just to stay alive," she said.

Julie and her husband had reliable work and a home, and they almost certainly were not captured in poverty statistics. But the despondency Julie exuded, and the lack of hope she seemed to have for her family, haunted me. The question, "Do you think the country is moving in the right direction?" seemed almost comically irrelevant when I asked it to open the conversation. The country had left her behind. Even if it was moving in the right direction, that wasn't going to help her.

In many cases, automation and globalization have eliminated jobs in certain industries altogether. As I continued down Julie's street, I struck up conversations with anyone I could find. (It helped that I was paired up with a young man from the host nonprofit who lived nearby.) In the span of a single hour's walk on a block in America's heartland, the effects of today's economic forces were on full display. Three doors down from Julie, we talked to a union pipe-layer who had been automated out of his last job and was trying to get retrained. A few houses further, a woman in her fifties had just been forced to retire early from the local department store, a victim of low consumer spending and ruthless price-gouging by the Walmart down the street. None of these people were poor, but all of their wages had stagnated or decreased in recent years. Many of the houses around them had been abandoned, or were in a state of near-total disrepair, evidence of a worse fate than wage stagnation.

Automation has destroyed jobs across America, particularly in communities like Warren. The jobs that disappeared first were the ones that required manual, routine labor, like in automobile manufacturing, historically one of the largest employers in the area. The world's largest automobile manufacturer, General Motors, made twice as many cars in 2011 as it made 55 years earlier with a third of the workforce. A single worker in 1955 made 8 cars; in 2011, 43.

To be sure, at the same time as technological advancements have destroyed jobs, they have created others, like Lyft drivers and Walmart workers. But the new jobs often require different skills, are unreliable, and pay worse. Walmart employees working less than 30 hours a week have no benefits, insurance, vacation, or paid leave, and what's more, they are lucky to make $15 an hour. That's a far cry from a factory worker who, at least in one region of Ohio, used to make $40 an hour or more, including the value of benefits. Automation may not have reduced the overall number of jobs, but the new jobs it has created are lower quality than the ones it has erased.

Meanwhile, globalization has similarly allowed enormous industries to move overseas. The economy of my hometown of Hickory has been decimated since furniture manufacturers moved production to China and the telecom industry downsized. These industries were the two major sources of employment when I was a kid, and they no longer exist. At the same time as robots made car assembly lines more efficient, trade agreements made it easier for the assembly of cars to move overseas. Meanwhile, private equity firms, a cousin of venture capital, bought up entire industries and squeezed short-term financial rewards out of them, caring little for companies' long-term performance.

All of these changes have introduced a profound confusion into the American psyche about the state of the

American Dream. We live in an age of overnight billion-aires, where anything seems possible, but economic opportunity is fading in many of our communities. There is a hope that the immense wealth created for the mega-winners might find its way to our children. But at the same time, a deep anger is simmering—a result of the growing sense that diligent hard work is not necessarily creating all this wealth.

We may not have realized we were creating this world over the past few decades, but we did. Our actions now can perpetuate it, or we can embrace more powerful instruments to combat the inequality we have produced.

3

KENYA

&

BACK

As a kid, I watched my parents dutifully tithe each year. They would tabulate their expected after-tax income and make a plan to give away 10 percent. Most of this money went to our church, but they set some aside to support local nonprofits and charities. They were exacting in how much they gave away and insisted that I follow their model with my $5 weekly allowance. I can remember my father regularly writing a check and stuffing it in a church envelope each week. As soon as I was old enough, I stuffed a few dollars into those envelopes once a month myself.

I took this tradition into adulthood and tithed a few thousand dollars every year out of my salaries from Facebook and the Obama campaign. And then, in the late summer of 2008, I sold $1 million of Facebook stock on the private markets. According to the math, I would need to give away $100,000 that year. I quickly realized I had no idea where I could put that kind of money with any confidence that it would make a lasting impact. A few years later, the challenge of effectively investing in the right causes became more complicated when, after Facebook's IPO, my husband and I decided to go beyond tithing and give away the vast majority of our newfound wealth over the course of our lifetimes.

It had been one thing to invest modest amounts in inspiring organizations working on important causes. It was self-evident, for instance, that we would become donors to the movement for marriage equality, which my husband worked on full time. But as we considered other causes to support, we found that we needed to make a distinction between those that seemed worthwhile—and there were many—and the ones that were the most critical to us in particular. As we added zeros to the amounts we were giving, choosing the right organizations and leaders became much more complex, charged, and important to get right. These investments could radically reshape organizations' trajectories and change people's lives. We wanted to make them carefully and thoughtfully. And we wanted to get the most bang for the buck—to do the most effective good with each additional dollar of investment.

One of the causes I decided to focus on was the fight to end extreme poverty internationally. What follows is the story of the journey I went on to explore the most effective ways to be helpful—and the surprising implications that work had for the economic challenges we face here at home. It is the story of how I came to believe in the potential of cash transfers in general, and the guaranteed income in particular, to empower people to chase their dreams.

It was approaching noon, and I was nauseous, hot, and restless. I was sitting in the back of a white Land Rover, bouncing along a dirt road in northeast Kenya somewhere near the Somali border. Our caravan of a half-dozen vehicles had set out from Nairobi before dawn, bound for a desert village called Dertu.

A year before, I had read a new book advancing a theory of how to help the billions of people who live on less than a dollar a day. Written by the economist and development expert Jeffrey Sachs, *The End of Poverty* was a blockbuster success. In it, he argued that if wealthy countries banded together to commit a small percentage of their economic output to anti-poverty work, the global community could end extreme poverty once and for all. He made the case that if we invest just enough money in a suite of social services like water purification, primary schooling, agricultural training, and rural electrification, economic development would follow. He dubbed the theory "integrated service delivery." Working in conjunction with the United Nations, his nonprofit had chosen 12 sites in Africa, called "Millennium Villages," to test the idea. The nomadic encampment at Dertu was one of these villages—in theory, a showpiece for what could happen if countries got serious about ending poverty. Sachs himself was in the Land Rover just ahead of ours, accompanied by several members of his team.

After driving for five hours, the caravan came to a stop amid a cloud of dust. In front of us was a collection of tin-roofed buildings with plain, brown cement walls that looked like they had grown up out of the desert along with the scrub surrounding them. The largest was long and narrow, like a barracks, and in front of the buildings was an open dirt field. A blue tarp had been set up off to the side as a kind of makeshift tent. As I climbed out of the vehicle, relieved to have two feet on the ground, a half-dozen Kenyans emerged from the shade of the blue tent and moved toward us. The women wore headscarves, and the men, standard Western clothing.

Dertu is in Kenya's North Eastern Province, which is effectively a slice of Somalia governed by Kenya. The border between the two countries is only 80 miles away, and like many of Africa's borders, it was drawn in the midst of the First World War with little consideration for the lives and cultures of the people on either side. The arbitrariness of the border was only outdone by the randomness of Dertu's founding. In 1997, UNICEF drilled a well in the middle of an arid stretch of desert for nomadic tribes to use, and Dertu had grown up around it.

Dertu's "residents" were the poorest people in one of the poorest regions of East Africa, and because of their nomadic lifestyle, some of the hardest to help. Sachs and the Millennium Village team had purposefully chosen to work there because of the challenge it represented. "What we're talking about here is a community that is barely surviving," Sachs told the journalist Nina Munk, who wrote a book on his work in the Millennium Villages in 2013. "Violent poverty, natural hazards, conflict, degradation of the environment—objectively speaking, it doesn't get harder than this."

The leader of the village, Ahmed Mohamed, walked over to greet us. A tall man with a short beard, he wore a traditional skullcap on his head. Several other village staff, looking joyous and relieved to see us, followed closely behind him. After a brief exchange of courtesies, they led us back to the tarp. As we sat cross-legged on traditional blankets, Ahmed and his team served us a lunch of fresh goat meat from a slaughter earlier in the day in honor of our arrival. They were especially deferential and courteous to Professor Sachs, whom they treated more like royalty than the academic economist I knew him to be. They clearly recognized that he had the power to change their lives.

By the time we finished our meal, word had spread that the *mzungu,* the white people, had arrived. Several dozen nomads surrounded us, smiling brightly. Only a few of them spoke English, but all of them wanted to catch a glimpse of Professor Sachs. We began our tour of the village just as the midday sun peaked in the sky and the temperature was pushing 100. Standing outside a small building that housed a new health clinic, we heard about the number of childbirths that were happening indoors instead of in the bush. We peered through the window at a sparse but organized dispensary, equipped with all the basics: sanitary gloves, syringes, an eye chart. Nothing was out of place; all appeared freshly cleaned and orderly.

From there, we moved to the dormitories, where the kids slept during the school year. Ahmed had convinced UNICEF to construct the simple buildings by making the case that having a place for children to sleep would encourage the nomadic herders to allow their young kids to stay in

Dertu for school. That barracks-like building, which had been completed just the year before, was the boys' dormitory. My stomach was roiling from the car ride or the goat, or some combination of the two. Desperate for relief from the sun, I peeled off from the group and walked inside, where it was much cooler. I could still hear Ahmed, and no one seemed to notice my absence. Curious to look around, I began to wander a bit on my own.

Something felt off. The clinic we had just seen had seemed a little too perfect, and this room felt a little too clean. I walked down a long aisle of bunk beds, each with a folded blanket atop it, one after another, perfectly ordered. I looked for any sign that people were actually sleeping here—for any trace of the dozens of young boys who in theory lived here year-round. Where were the personal items that schoolkids have, even the poorest of the poor? There were no pencils, no bars of soap, no papers—not even a scrap of clothing. There were no signs of life. It was more like a movie set than a kids' dorm.

I went back outside and waited for Ahmed to finish speaking. The group peeked into the building through a window and started to move on. I approached Ahmed as we walked. "Where is the stuff?" I asked him quietly. He seemed not to understand. "Where is the kids' personal stuff? Pencils, books—that kind of thing? There was nothing in the dormitory."

"We cleaned it before you came," he replied while nodding. I nodded back and kept walking. It was true—the room had looked recently swept and tidied. Maybe I was wrong, and I just didn't understand the real depth of poverty in Dertu.

Next up was a small schoolhouse. We learned that the teacher had formerly traveled to nearby pastoralist encampments to teach, but since the dormitories had been built, it was possible for him to centralize his work in Dertu. The classroom was extremely sparse, but it was stocked with basic items—chalk, erasers, books, and simple desks. But yet again, there was no sign of life or the presence of any actual children. The teacher stood at the front of the classroom, smiling and nodding, and told us about how flexible and modern the curriculum was.

We walked down the hall and stopped beside a single computer sitting on a desk behind a grill and padlock protecting it. Professor Sachs turned to me to make sure I was paying attention to the tech part of the tour—had this been prepped especially for me? The teacher told us how miraculous it was that Sony had donated several computers to the school. Ericsson had built a cell phone tower nearby, and thanks to those two gifts, the wealth and knowledge of the entire Internet could be tapped by his students. I was intrigued. I asked, this time in front of the whole group, "Is it the teachers or the kids who use the computers?"

"Both, but mostly the teachers," the teacher answered.

"What do you use it for?" I asked him.

"Everything. We use it for everything," he replied.

At first I thought there might just be a breakdown in translation. If you weren't fluent in English, you might give such a broad and ambiguous answer to a hard question. But both Ahmed and the teacher spoke English well.

I was becoming increasingly suspicious. This computer was literally locked up, even on the day of the tour. The Internet connection, if it had one, would be a slow and unreliable one via the cell phone tower or satellite. Either way, it would make the Internet extremely difficult to use. I loved the idea of nomads in the Somali desert exploring the world through their Google searches, but it seemed nearly unbelievable that an Internet built for the West would be of much day-to-day use to the people here, if it worked at all.

"What kind of things in particular do you do?" I pressed him.

"We use it for all kinds of things."

"Can you give me an example?" He looked confused, so one of the white Millennium Village program staffers volunteered that they used it for things like "lesson plan development." I was bordering on obnoxious, but I had come halfway across the world, so I persisted. "What kind of sites or resources do you use for lesson plan development?" I asked the teacher. A look of panic crossed his face.

"We can follow up with that kind of info afterward," the white staffer interjected once more. Others started to shift uncomfortably, but no one said anything. The tour continued.

When Nina Munk later visited the village, she discovered that the computers had never been connected to the Internet, and all of them were eventually stolen.

The rest of the afternoon was full of similarly upbeat and evasive claims. Everything was going "extremely well," but nothing seemed right. The Millennium Village felt more and more like a Potemkin Village to me. Finally, after spending just two or three hours in Dertu, we returned to the Land Rovers and departed. I left with more questions than answers, and over the next couple of years, I got them.

Almost from the beginning, the project had been beset by controversy. A series of papers published just after my visit in 2010 called into question the Millennium Village's marketing materials. Its annual reports claimed "remarkable progress" and cited lower incidences of HIV and malarial infections, lower child mortality rates, and more educational opportunities. But researchers at the Center for Global Development at the World Bank noted that it was impossible to measure the villages' impact, because there was no "control," or empirical baseline, to compare it to. Malarial and HIV infection rates had been falling in neighboring villages too, and educational opportunities had been expanded in those places as well. Though Sachs disputed these claims, much of the development community grew skeptical of the project. The lead economist at the World Bank's development group called Sachs's assertions of the impact "baffling." A year later, the director of monitoring and evaluation for the Millennium Villages was forced to resign after he was caught manipulating data to claim that the child mortality rate was decreasing three times faster in Millennium Villages than it was in Kenya as a whole.

Five years after the project began in Dertu, despite millions of dollars of corporate and government philanthropy, Dertu had no paved roads, electricity, or running water. Its latrines were full; garbage was piled high. The members of the community filed a 14-point complaint with the local member of parliament. Sachs raised an additional $70 million to extend his project in some of the other villages, but the Millennium Villages website says that work in Dertu was "completed" in 2011. And yet for all that, the project's 2010 annual report claimed a "stunning transformation of 500,000 lives."

The Millennium Villages have been one of the most expensive and troubled interventions in Africa, yet the nonprofit behind the villages, Millennium Promise, has a three-star rating (out of four possible) on Charity Navigator, a website that helps donors make informed decisions about which nonprofits to support. Over the past decade, Millennium Promise has raised nearly $200 million. Its branding book provides guidelines for how to present its logo, and its annual report and website show smiling faces, positive statistics, and specific results. It looks and feels like just about every other nonprofit brochure you have seen. Looking at it from the outside, you would have no idea how ineffective and discredited the model is. The failure of the Millennium Village Project was not because Professor Sachs and the team didn't have the best of intentions. It's hard not to be humbled by their dedication to the cause; they are some of the most driven, caring, and generous people on the planet. But good intentions and the smartest of expert interventions alone are not enough to transform lives.

The Millennium Villages came to represent for me an approach to combating economic injustice and poverty that was about engineering progress from the top down, rather than respecting the agency and autonomy of the people you set out to empower. In this approach, foreign experts assume that interventions as simple and superficially laudable as digging a well or building a school will improve the lives of the people they are meant to serve. But every culture and place presents unique and often hidden challenges, and a lot of money and energy can be wasted quickly. An expert's plan hatched in Nairobi or New York might sound good and look attractive to a donor in a colorful brochure, but that doesn't mean it will work or improve people's lives thousands of miles away.

To be clear, some of the other Millennium Villages fared better than Dertu. The second village in Kenya, called Sauri, has produced more meaningful results: increased agricultural output, more children in school, and fewer people infected with malaria. Aid interventions can occasionally work, but the question is, at what cost? What else could we be funding with those dollars? If we could help and empower the poor more effectively and more cheaply, why wouldn't we? I began to wonder if a different kind of approach that embraces the decision-making power of the beneficiaries and invests in them directly might not only be more respectful of the communities served, but more impactful. As a person looking to invest every dollar as effectively as possible, this seemed to me to be the most important and urgent question to ask.

In the year after that trip to Kenya, I began work on a nonprofit start-up called Jumo. Our goal was to help nonprofits in the United States and around the globe publicize their work and connect with new donors and volunteers. We created a social network for causes, and 5,000 nonprofits signed up. As we built the network, I began to feel that we were playing the role of a marketing channel for the charities, which had nothing to do with how effective they might be. Unlike in the private sector, where a store owner knows she's doing well when a lot of people buy her goods, nonprofits don't have the same feedback loop. The number of donations that come in is not necessarily correlated with the quality of work the charity is doing, but instead is tied to how well the nonprofit leaders sell their causes.

Marketing science manipulates well-intentioned potential donors by telling them that their gifts will be matched or by showing a heart-wrenching photo of a child with a fly on her nose. The charities are not doing anything wrong—over time, they have developed a playbook to convert sympathy into contributions. Those donations pay their bills. But the natural result of this structure is that organizations put more and more emphasis on effective fund-raising, and less emphasis on assessing whether the programs they are administering are effective. Few nonprofit groups invest the time and resources to have independent third parties verify their impact. My lesson from the Millennium Villages in Dertu was to never assume that good intentions mean real impact, even if the people at work are sincere and knowledgeable.

Without realizing it at first, I had created in Jumo yet another marketing channel for charities to sell themselves, when what I should have been doing was finding a better way to assess their effectiveness. I quickly became disillusioned and decided to merge Jumo into another online network. I began to focus more narrowly on the question of how I could invest the wealth that was still building from Facebook into a cause that I could be sure would have an impact. I was on the hunt for something verifiably helpful—something that didn't just make for good marketing.

Late one evening, I discovered several blog posts on the website of a group called GiveWell that one of its founders had written during a trip to India. I knew the author, Holden Karnofsky, because he and his colleague Elie Hassenfeld had sublet a few desks in our shared office space a year earlier. Before starting GiveWell, Elie and Holden had been associates at Bridgewater, one of the largest hedge funds in the world. Their challenge was similar to mine: they wanted to use the same rigorous methods they had used to evaluate a financial opportunity for their hedge fund to assess the charities they were considering donating to. "We scoured the Internet, but couldn't find the answers to our questions, either through charities' own websites or through the foundations that fund them," they wrote when they started GiveWell. They made it their mission to do research and due diligence for themselves and other donors on how to make their giving as impactful as it could possibly be.

One of the blog posts I read that night offered a short and pithy reflection on the age-old question that many of us have struggled with at some point: Should I give money to a person begging in the street? Holden had gone to India and, in the face of rampant poverty and homelessness, found himself wondering if he should just pass out money. On my first trip to India years before, dozens of children, no more than five or six years old, had encircled me, tapping my legs and hands. Their plaintive, unwashed faces and persistent requests for "chapatti, chapatti, chapatti," the word for a simple bread, had never left me. "Here, more than in NYC," Holden wrote, "I could arguably carry out a mini 'cash transfer' program on my own. The question is whether I should." His provocation stuck in my head.

Holden's question of whether he could run his own "cash transfer" program, shorthand for just giving people cash directly, wasn't just a passing curiosity. The GiveWell team and he felt a responsibility to investigate what it would mean to do exactly that, just as they ran down every single other way of giving to assess its impact. As GiveWell grew, it became an anchor for the "effective altruism" movement, a philanthropic approach moving away from pull-the-heartstrings inspiration and toward empirical, transparent, and rigorous evaluation of impact. The Princeton philosopher Peter Singer pioneered this utilitarian approach to philanthropy, and not without controversy. "By donating a relatively small amount of money, you could save a child's life," he writes in *The Life You Can Save*. "Maybe it takes more than the amount needed to buy a pair of shoes—but we all spend money on things we don't really need, whether on drinks, meals out, clothing, movies, concerts, vacations, new cars, or house renovation. Is it possible that by choosing to spend your money on such things rather than contributing to an aid agency, you are leaving a child to die, a child you could have saved?" Singer, GiveWell, and the effective altruism movement are in pursuit of a practical ethics that seeks not just to give away money, but to rethink our collective responsibility to one another and create a tradition in philanthropy focused on maximizing the return of each dollar invested.

Holden's post only came to tentative initial conclusions, but I marveled at the simplicity of the idea of giving cash directly. My curiosity grew over the course of weeks and then months. Why was my default to trust an educated outsider or nonprofit executive with resources rather than the poor themselves? The radical, irreverent nature of the idea that the poor might know the best way to solve their own problems hit a nerve. It connected to my natural skepticism of people in power that my parents had inculcated in me from a young age and which had only grown with exposure to the professional nonprofit infrastructure I had witnessed in places like Dertu. What if the most effective way to help somebody might be to get all those experts intent on over-engineering progress out of the way?

A couple years later, I found myself back in Kenya for another predawn trip into the bush. The day before, I had flown from New York to London, from London to Nairobi, and from Nairobi to the city of Kisumu. Despite being only seven miles from the equator, the mountain air that morning was crisp and cool. This time there was no caravan outside the hotel—just a single white van. I jumped in and joined the half-dozen other passengers, who worked for a nonprofit called GiveDirectly. I sat in the first row, and GiveDirectly's CEO Michael Faye, a brown-haired, wiry man in his thirties, sat beside me. We set out on a two-hour ride to a group of villages near a town called Siaya.

An hour into the trip, the van popped a tire. We pulled over to the side of the road and filed out one by one. We all milled about awkwardly while the driver hauled out a spare and the equipment to change the tire. The swap did not look like it was going to happen quickly. Michael, uninterested in wasting time on such an important day, took a few steps away in frustration. Shuffling about, he turned around and looked at the group. "Should we just rent motorbikes for the last 20 miles?" he asked. "We'd probably get there faster anyway, and we could see more."

I assumed he was joking, but all of a sudden the local staff were saying, "Let's do it!" I looked at a colleague who had accompanied me across the world. Her look back at me confirmed that they were indeed crazy. "How about we give it 15 minutes instead?" I said. We bought a Fanta from a shack nearby and settled in.

This was my third trip to Kenya and my second to the GiveDirectly villages. My first had happened a year earlier. After I read Holden's blog post, my curiosity about cash transfers had grown quickly. Over the next several months, I had followed every lead I could find into the world of "cash assistance." It turned out there was an entire field dedicated to the topic, and several books and hundreds of reports had been written about experimental cash transfer programs all over the world. Michael and another economist, Paul Niehaus, had recently started GiveDirectly to enable American donors to give cash away to those who needed it most. While working on their PhDs at Harvard, they had grown suspicious of the effectiveness of many aid programs. Hundreds of studies and their own instincts told them that cash might be a more powerful tool to help the poor than traditional programs, but no American charity would allow them to give directly to the people most in need.

They decided to do it themselves. In 2010, they began distributing their own money to families—$1,000 to each, with no strings attached—who lived in the slums around Nairobi on less than a dollar a day. They incorporated

GiveDirectly as a charity the same year and began raising money from outside donors as well. I connected with Michael and Paul soon after, through what was then GiveDirectly's extremely basic website. Paul, an award-winning economist, moonlighted as a coder and had built the website himself. Light on photos, heavy on statistics, and generally clunky, it was the exact opposite of every nonprofit website I had seen over the previous few years, and I loved it. Clearly, they were uninterested in marketing, and they had no plan for donor cultivation or management. They scoffed at the idea of a gala or a glossy annual report and questioned everything about the traditional nonprofit model. They purposefully made themselves unappealing to the vast majority of donors so they could focus on a smaller set that valued performance over pop. Within months, I gave my first $100,000, and GiveDirectly in turn sent $90,000 of that—via text message—to 90 families who had been living on less than $1 a day. (They limit staff costs and overhead to 10 percent of each dollar given.) This was as close to literally handing out money as I could come.

An hour after the van had gotten underway again, it pulled over to the side of the road. There were no huts in sight, and no evidence of human civilization outside of a few Kenyan women carrying parcels and walking alongside the road. The local staff member who had organized the expedition hopped out of the van, gestured toward the horizon, and said, "This way!" She set out, and the rest of us fell in line behind her.

After a 20-minute walk through the bush, brambles nipping at our legs, we finally arrived at a set of red-earth huts. All of the people who lived in this tiny village had received cash transfers over the past year—two payments of roughly $500, made via M-Pesa, a mobile service that enables easy money transfers. The digital money can be converted to traditional paper currency at any time. The villages that GiveDirectly serves are not directly connected to paved roads, and most do not have basic infrastructure like electricity or running water. Most of the villagers are engaged in subsistence farming and fishing.

When GiveDirectly takes donors or journalists on tours of these villages, they don't prescreen recipients to prepare and package the best stories, but instead choose the huts at random. You don't always meet the most talkative people or hear the most riveting stories, and a lot of times, no one is home. But instead of marketing pizzazz, you see a more representative sample of the beneficiaries, and you know that you are not just being sold a bill of goods.

We split up into two groups so as not to overwhelm the recipients. My group ducked into a hut with a new aluminum roof (most of the huts we had seen on the walk over were thatched). The woman who sat across from us was nearly six feet tall and wore a simple cotton dress, yellow plastic sandals, and had a scarf tied on top of her head. She was very quiet, almost whispering her responses to our questions. She had lived in the hut for a decade, she told us, and her husband spent much of his time fishing on Lake

Victoria. Her children were grown. They had used half of their transfer to replace their thatch roof with aluminum. The average amount saved in ongoing repair costs was $110 annually, meaning their investment would pay off in a few years. She had used the rest of the transfer for food and as a gift to her kids.

We had similar conversations in the next two homes we visited. Another family had installed a solar-powered light-bulb in their hut so their kids could do schoolwork in the evenings. One recipient said to us, through the translator, that another charity had given him a cow. "What am I going to do with a cow? Now I have to feed it and take care of it!" He didn't need or want livestock, but a charity had decided that he should have it, regardless of his interest or ability to maintain it. All of the homes had different-color chalk markings on the doors, evidence of all of the other nonprofits who had come through at one point or another with some kind of service to provide or good to give out. Where were they now?

Another recipient our companions talked to that day, a young bachelor, was the entrepreneurial type. Saturday nights in Kenya, like Saturday nights in a lot of other places in the world, are a time to rest and unwind after a busy week. Friends of his threw parties or celebrations with so-das, sweets, and beer. They used a small radio to play music, but the sound was often scrambled with static. He believed he could do better, so he used his first transfer to buy a keyboard. It enabled him to perform as a musician and DJ, and he charged the partygoers a small fee. With the second transfer he invested in an unrelated and similarly creative idea. He spent some of the money on livestock and used the rest to buy a beehive. Everybody wanted fresh and cheap honey, and he didn't mind the occasional beesting. His apiary provided him another independent revenue stream.

In contrast to the integrated service delivery model in the Millennium Villages, with its costly overhead and UN-approved white papers, GiveDirectly was doing something painfully simple and obvious: letting the people in need decide for themselves. Village residents could pool their money to build a well, use the funds for school fees, or invest in their homes. Not every decision would be wise, but it seemed like this kind of investment respected their local knowledge and their ability to direct their own lives.

And the evidence shows that on balance, cash transfers like these are more effective at improving the lives of the communities they serve than other aid interventions. In 2011, GiveDirectly's leadership enlisted independent researchers affiliated with MIT's Poverty Action Lab to assess the impact of their transfers. The analysis was done in coordination with the independent nonprofit Innovations for Poverty Action and the National Institutes of Health. The study analyzed the impact of cash transfers using a randomized control trial, the same methodology that pharmaceutical companies use to assess the power of a new drug and its side effects. The researchers surveyed recipients before they received the money to establish a baseline and again afterward to understand the impact. They then compared those villages to a set of "control" villages that did not receive transfers. The design of the study was pre-announced so it was impossible to bury unflattering data, and the researchers opened their raw data sets to the world. They even paid independent researchers to comb through it to find errors or inconsistencies.

Even though the study had a relatively short time horizon of two years, the researchers documented significant positive effects on the cash recipients' assets, earnings, food security, mental health, and female empowerment. The income of families increased by 27 percent, and the value of the assets that they held, like livestock and their homes, increased by $430, a significant amount for people who live on less than a dollar a day. Additional spending on nutrition significantly reduced the families' food insecurity index, a measurement of meals skipped and diet quality.

Perhaps most importantly, the recipients were happier. The researchers used a psychological well-being index that was a weighted average of the participants' responses to an internationally standardized questionnaire. They found a significant increase in self-reported life satisfaction. A reporter at *Business Insider* summarized the results: "People who received the money were happier, more satisfied with life, less stressed, and depressed less often."

The researchers also found that recipients of the benefit, along with their neighbors who did not receive the benefit but lived in the same village, scored higher on a female empowerment index that measures things like domestic violence rates and attitudes toward men. They are now doing a longer-term assessment to see if they can replicate the outcome, but these studies suggest that having more economic security lowers the overall stress level in a home and the rate of domestic violence.

Interestingly, the study showed no increase in the amount of alcohol and tobacco consumed. Skeptical that participants would give an honest answer to the question, the researchers used a different methodology to assess the use of these so-called temptation goods. They presented a list of five common activities, like talking on the phone or visiting friends, and then asked how many of these activities the respondents had done in the past week. One group was presented with a list that did not include alcohol and tobacco, another with the list plus alcohol, and a third with the list plus tobacco. The question the respondents answered was, "Have you participated in any of these five activities in the past week?" and the respondents did not need to specify which, if any, they had. The researchers compared the responses across different groups and found no increased likelihood that cash recipients consumed more alcohol or tobacco than the control group.

GiveDirectly's study is a drop in the research bucket when it comes to cash. Over the past few decades, nearly 200 other studies have been conducted on 56 different kinds of cash transfer programs, and they have produced a variety of results based on the amount and frequency of the transfer, who receives it, and how long they receive it for. A recent review of all of these studies by the Overseas Development Institute found several consistent effects: cash transfers reduce immediate poverty and increase savings, raise school attendance, cause recipients to use health services more frequently, and are associated with a reduction in child labor. Most studies show no effect on the amount of time adults work, and some show people work more. Another review of all cash studies by the World Bank showed no evidence that cash transfers affect drinking or smoking behavior.

Aid organizations like the International Rescue Committee (IRC) and World Food Programme (WFP) have caught on. Over the past five years, WFP has migrated a massive portion of its budget, nearly $900 million in 2016, to providing people cash rather than bowls of rice. "WFP takes the view that it is the people it serves who are in a position to decide what is best for them," the organization says in its review of the power of cash. "Cash-based transfers help by giving the purchasing power to the people." The IRC has similarly put cash allowances at the center of how it responds to refugee crises across the world, providing cash to Iraqi families newly liberated from ISIS and refugees from the Middle East and North Africa stranded in Greece. It has committed to distribute a quarter of its humanitarian aid as cash transfers by 2020, up from around 6 percent when the announcement was made in 2015.

The amount of cash benefits that humanitarian organizations provide is still small, but it has grown by a factor of five in a little more than a decade. At the same time, American donors interested in extreme poverty have gotten behind GiveDirectly's work. In 2012, when I began donating, the organization raised $500,000 total. In 2015 and 2016, GiveDirectly raised more than $90 million to fund its programs.

A sea change in international development is reshaping the sector. In the year after I returned from Africa, I watched as the idea caught fire. The GiveDirectly experiments had been one catalyst, but other cash programs in Brazil and Mexico had sparked a robust conversation about the best way to help the poor and middle class in developing economies. Iran cashed in all of its complex food and energy subsidies to create the first nationwide cash transfer program, and India is considering doing the same. The IRC began to pilot cash transfer programs in disaster and humanitarian relief zones, and global think tanks produced new reports assessing the power of cash to transform lives. Most of the analyses came to the same conclusion: cash is one of the most powerful ways to lift people out of poverty. It is not a panacea, but in many cases, it should be the centerpiece of aid programs in conjunction with other supports like schools and hospitals.

At the same time that cash was becoming increasingly ascendant in international circles, I was paying more attention to the brewing economic problems in the United States. The United States has little in common with a country like Kenya, where GiveDirectly works. Our economy is 265 times larger, and our government and social services are significantly more robust. It feels like a stretch to compare the work of a small international nonprofit like GiveDirectly to American government programs.

But as I grew increasingly inspired by the power of cash internationally, I wondered how cash transfers might beat back the economic forces that had created historic inequality in our own country. The scale of the problem was much larger and more expensive, and I quickly realized that any long-term solution would need to shift public policy and not just rely on philanthropy to reach everyone who needed it.

To my surprise, I discovered that the United States already runs the biggest cash transfer program in the world, giving tens of billions of dollars, no strings attached, to struggling poor families to help boost their incomes and stabilize their financial lives. We don't talk about it much, but we have good, home-grown evidence that aligns with the international studies' conclusions: that this money is well spent and lifts education and health outcomes for recipients here, just as it does abroad. And by tweaking and expanding it, we could make it possible for all American families to make ends meet.

4

THE

PRECARIAT

Over the past couple years, many technology and business leaders have come to believe we need a guaranteed income because of the threat of artificial intelligence. Elon Musk and Richard Branson, for instance, believe that "intelligent" machines may soon create a new era of mass unemployment. In that world, they argue, there will be no choice but to help people meet their basic needs.

These leaders aren't contemplating a future of whole-sale job destruction in order to be contrarian or controversial. They see a meaningful difference between the impacts of emerging artificial intelligence and the automation we have already come to know. Whereas automation is what we generally think of with technology—robotic arms and ATMs—artificial intelligence is the capacity for algorithms or machines to learn for themselves. They are increasingly able to incorporate feedback from their actions and to adjust future behavior, simulating a kind of intelligence. For instance, Facebook's photo software will scan a photo you took, match it to its existing database, and then suggest that you tag that photo "Mom." When you give it an answer, "Yes, that's my Mom," or "No, that's not her," it incorporates whether or not it got its initial prediction right into the algorithm that powered the initial match. Next time it will know better if a person with that facial structure is "Mom." The same goes with Google's translation software or Amazon's Echo devices, which are constantly incorporating feedback into their future performance plans. Tesla's self-driving cars improve their driving ability by collecting, storing, and analyzing all of the driving data they receive while cars are on the road. These systems aren't just automating processes: they are growing smarter over time.

There is little doubt that artificial intelligence *could* destroy many jobs in the future, but I'm not sure they will. Self-driving cars could replace human drivers, and smart bots might replace personal assistants. The white-collar jobs of doctors and nurses, teachers, and lawyers might be radically reshaped with the introduction of smarter technologies. But all of these things fall in the category of "might" happen, and there are plenty of experts who believe there is little reason to believe in the hype of artificial intelligence. They do not believe the claims that "this time is different."

Before President Barack Obama left office, I was a guest at a small dinner in Washington, D.C., at the Brookings Institution, a well-respected policy think tank. I was the youngest guest in the room by far, and the only one not wearing the Washington uniform of suit and tie. Jason Furman, then the chair of the president's Council of Economic Advisers, was discussing "digital competitiveness" in today's economy. Midway through Furman's presentation, I found an opening to ask, "What are you doing to plan for a future with more artificial intelligence where there might be fewer jobs?" He paused, barely concealing his annoyance with such a predictable question, coming from such a predictable source, even though I was skeptical of the claim myself. "Three hundred years of economic history tells us that can't be true," he said curtly. It was the only question he answered that night with a single sentence. This is one area of rare agreement between the Obama economic team and Donald Trump's administration. Steve Mnuchin, Trump's treasury secretary, said last year that he was "not at all" worried about job displacement at the hands of technology. "In terms of artificial intelligence taking American jobs, I think we're, like, so far away from that—not even on my radar screen," Mnuchin said. "I think it's 50 or 100 more years."

Nine out of ten economists, a University of Chicago survey found, agree with Furman and Mnuchin. As Furman later explained it in a seminal speech, "Over long periods of time it has generally been the case that about 95 percent of the people in the United States who want a job at a given point in time can find one—despite massive changes in technology." Workers, technologists, and politicians have indeed often cried wolf, going back to the dawn of the Industrial Revolution. During the Luddite uprisings in early nineteenth-century England, weavers destroyed the automated looms that were threatening their livelihoods. A century and a half later, in the 1950s and 1960s, early computers raised concerns among policymakers and business leaders that mass unemployment was just around the bend. A report written by prominent academics, journalists, and technologists called the "Triple Revolution" foresaw a world of historic inequality as machines dramatically increased industrial output and required "little cooperation with human beings." In response to the report, President Lyndon Johnson convened a National Commission on Technology, Automation, and Economic Progress to prepare for a robot future. Yet over the decade that followed, the American economy created 18 million new jobs, many of them unheard of before.

There are days when I talk to a technologist in the morning, who is convinced that the end of work is looming, and in the afternoon to an academic, who believes nothing has changed. They may not always realize it, but there is a lot of room for agreement between the camps if they focus on what we know. Technology has already changed the nature of work. Incomes are stagnant and unpredictable, and fewer and fewer people are able to do better than their parents, while the cost of living keeps rising. The debate about artificial intelligence is in large part irrelevant to why we need a guaranteed income today: we are already experiencing one of the most significant economic dislocations in modern history.

We don't need to predict the future to know that we need to respond to the problems of the economy of the present. Regardless of how artificial intelligence evolves, a guaranteed income is the best tool to provide financial stability and opportunity to people who already need it.

To understand how our new economy, defined by technological advances and globalization, affects the bottom lines of working people, two researchers, Rachel Schneider and James Morduch, set out to monitor the day-to-day financial behavior of 235 low- and middle-income families over the course of a year. They tracked all money in, all money out, what they spent it on, and why. They combined that data set with anonymized statements from Chase bank accounts to create an even larger sample. The top-line conclusion from their work: while income inequality gets a lot of attention, financial instability and the challenges that come with weathering the ups and downs of unpredictable income are just as problematic, if not more so.

I worked with a woman on the Obama campaign who lived that instability every year. A Chicago local, she didn't have a fancy educational pedigree or deep campaign experience, but for all that her resume lacked, she had a dedication and passion that matched or exceeded everyone else's to put her senator in the White House. I remember one night in the campaign office, after almost everyone had left, she told me what her life had been like over the past several years. She worked at the Navy Pier, a local amusement park, from May to September and took as many hours as she could. When the pier closed in the fall, she turned to odd jobs, babysitting, and any kind of temp work she could find, scrounging and saving until spring came around again. Technically, she had an income for much of the year, and while I don't know for sure, she probably did not appear in any poverty statistics. She lived right on the brink, one month to another, hoping for no major setbacks. She is one of the tens of millions of temporary workers this economy has created.

Headlines tell us that unemployment numbers keep hitting record lows in the United States, but these numbers mask the human effects of precarious work.

My colleague and people like her live in a precarity trap that Schneider and Morduch describe in their work. "Without basic economic stability," Schneider and Morduch write, "their choices are often difficult, and they're forced to make them frequently. Short-term imperatives undermine long-term goals. Saving and borrowing need to be recalibrated with the spikes and dips of their income. The consequences of bad decisions can compound, and quickly. Stress and anxiety make it all harder."

In a separate study, the Pew Research Center asked more than 7,000 Americans to balance the trade-off between reliable income and more income. Nine out of ten said they would rather be paid less and have the money arrive regularly. Most of the people in these studies, like most Americans today, can find some kind of paid work, but the kinds of jobs that are available to them fail to provide the security of a reliable income.

A hundred and fifty million Americans are living from paycheck to paycheck, and it isn't because they aren't trying hard enough. Some might wonder, are they just not saving? Are they buying too many new gadgets and fancy cars when they should be diligently socking money away into a rainy day fund? Almost to a fault, every poor and middle-class person in these studies was attempting to build a nest egg. Nearly all the participants had savings accounts and many of them thought up ways to make it harder for them to touch that money. One woman in Mississippi purposefully opened a savings account in a credit union an hour's drive away from her home. She cut up her ATM card to make it harder to withdraw money from it, and she destroyed her checkbook so she wouldn't be tempted by payday loans, which often require a signed check as collateral. Despite many similar stories of thoughtfulness and preparation from the families interviewed for the study, few of the participants managed to create long-term savings because of unpredictable life events like collapses in wages, hospitalizations, or unexpected childcare costs.

If instability has become the new norm, a second effect of the winner-take-all economy on workers' lives is the absence of economic mobility, the chance to get ahead. My parents and their parents before them felt, like most Americans, a confidence that their kids would be better off than they were. Incomes rose in the United States in every decade leading up to the Great Depression, and then again in the decades that followed. Jobs were changing with every decade, but pay was consistently rising.

Across the board today, it has become less likely that people born into poor or middle-class households will move up the economic ladder. In the America of the 1950s, a child had a nine-out-of-ten chance of making more money than their parents, but today it is only 50 percent. Today, a child born into poverty in France has a better chance of entering the highest social classes than one born in the United

States. The majority of middle-class Americans today are stuck where they are—or they are falling. "If you're in the middle, you're stuck in the middle, which means there's less space for others to move into the middle," says Elisabeth Jacobs, the senior director for policy and academic programs at the Washington Center for Equitable Growth. As jobs have become increasingly unreliable, they don't offer the same chance to move up and out that they once did.

We shouldn't let nostalgia for the good old days of economic mobility allow us to forget that it was largely only one class of Americans, white men, who were able to take advantage of available economic opportunities. Policymakers across the country and in Washington consistently made decisions that made it easier for whites to get ahead and harder for minorities, particularly African Americans. Few African Americans were able to take advantage of early social assistance programs like the Homestead Act, which gave each settler 160 acres in exchange for a commitment to work the land. African Americans were denied access to many of the land grant colleges that provided free education to farmers who wanted it. (Most Southern universities refused to admit African Americans until the late 1960s.) Later, in the middle of the twentieth century, the GI Bill provided service members returning home after the Second World War with low-interest loans and low-cost mortgages, but only to those who were white. Banks for most of American history refused to lend to African Americans, even well after the passage of the Civil Rights Act. Similarly, elected officials made it difficult for women to purchase and own property for much of American history. Women lacked access to many professional schools, like law schools and medical schools, and the financially rewarding careers that result. Even today, men are paid consistently more in jobs than women who do the exact same work, and we have no national paid leave policies to help new parents, particularly mothers, balance work with children. We don't need to go back in time and "make America great again" by re-creating a world that provided economic mobility to a select group—we need to build a new economic order that empowers all Americans to get ahead.

A third and final effect of the new economy on working people is an exorbitant and growing cost of living. The NPR show *Marketplace,* in collaboration with *Frontline* and PBS *NewsHour,* crunched the data on the cost of everything from fast food to health care and movie tickets to gas between 1995 and 2015. Their finding was conclusive: "Middle-class life has become 30 percent more expensive in the past 20 years. In that same time, Americans haven't received a raise."

The rise in expense of three essentials—housing, health care, and education—accounts for the bulk of the cost explosion. Even after adjusting for inflation, college tuition fees are two and a half times what they were 20 years ago, while the costs of childcare and medical care are double what they were in 1997. Housing, food, and energy costs are similarly 50 percent more expensive than they were then. (The only things that have gotten much cheaper are television sets, toys, and software.) The "production" of things like health care, education, and housing has not gotten meaningfully more efficient through automation or globalization, because they all rely on cognitive human labor, which is harder to automate or ship overseas than manufacturing processes. You might be able to buy a less expensive television made in a Chinese factory, but you can't save money by sending your kids to a preschool in Beijing.

Unfortunately, these trends show no signs of slowing down. As state and federal governments tighten their belts, tuition and medical expenses are trending upward. While artificial intelligence will likely bring down the cost of some goods, costs will likely continue to rise in the industries that most rely on human expertise like education and health care. Business journalist Jordan Weissmann points out that "prices are rising on the very things that are essential for climbing out of poverty. A college education has become a necessary passport to financial stability. It's hard to hold a job if you're chronically ill. Working full-time is difficult if you can't pay somebody to watch your child."

A high cost of living is not just a problem for the poor— the cost squeeze affects most of the middle class as well. The poor struggle to pay heating bills and make rent. While the middle class may not be going to bed hungry, the rising costs of housing, health care, and education mean many of them live on the financial brink.

We rely on the monthly job report with fresh unemployment numbers to gauge how well the economy is doing for working people, but it says nothing about these hidden problems that many employed people still have. In a world in which a job meant stability and opportunity, it made sense to look at the number of jobs as a barometer of how well people were faring in the economy. Lots of people today have a job but do not have any semblance of financial security in their lives. There's a reason we have a reactionary president who leverages populist rhetoric at a time of record-low unemployment. We have the power to fix these problems by creating an income floor to support and stabilize the lives of poor and working-class Americans.

5

A GUARANTEED INCOME FOR WORKING PEOPLE

Here's what I propose we do. Government should provide a guaranteed income of $500 a month to every adult who lives in a household making less than $50,000 per year and who is working in some way. This would add up to $6,000 a year for a single person or $12,000 for a married couple. A family of four making $38,000 a year would see their annual income rise to $50,000, a huge boost to their bottom line. A single worker at Walmart who works 25 hours a week for $10 an hour would see her income increase from $13,000 to $19,000.

The guaranteed income would create a floor below which people could not fall, a reliable foundation for people to build on. It wouldn't be enough money on its own for anyone to live on. It would supplement income from other sources like formal labor, a job in the gig economy, informal work, or other government benefits. Everyone who contributes to their community would earn the income, even if they're not making money in the formal economy. That would include mothers and fathers of young kids, adults caring for aging parents, and college students.

A fruit picker or Lyft driver would have a monthly cash stipend they could plan on, even if it were a bad season or if fewer people needed rides one particular month. A student would have a foundation to be able to pursue her studies full time, and a mother with young kids would have extra cash to help with the cost of diapers and clothes. A guaranteed income would stabilize erratic financial lives and give people extra cash to invest in themselves and their families.

A guaranteed income of this size would lift 20 million out of poverty overnight and provide financial stability to many in the middle class. It would give people the chance to invest in themselves to start a small business, or to move to a new city for a new job. It would help people keep up with the rising cost of living. They could spend the money on whatever was most important to them—housing, health care, education, childcare, or something else. But perhaps most importantly, the guaranteed income would embrace the dignity and freedom of people to chase their own dreams with no restrictions.

Anyone who made more than $50,000 would not get the money, because they have enough income to make ends meet. (This amount would be adjusted by the cost of living in each state: in California it would be a bit higher, and in Alabama, it would be lower.) But no one in the middle class would pay for it either. A tax on the incomes of the richest Americans, those who make more than $250,000 a year, would underwrite the program in its entirety.

A guaranteed income of this size would provide 60 million adults with monthly checks, at a new annual cost of $290 billion, about half of what we spend each year on defense. It's important to be clear about the scale of this program: it would be big and expensive. It would be the fourth-largest social benefit in government, just behind Social Security, Medicare, and Medicaid. This level of spending is ambitious, but it's feasible if we have the political will to do it. We could begin more modestly and scale the program up over time, just as we've done with other programs, like Social Security. When President Franklin Roosevelt signed the first Social Security bill, it barely covered half of the working population, but it grew over decades to cover virtually every American. We could start the guaranteed income at $150 per month, taking the cost down dramatically to less than $50 billion, and then increase it gradually over time. Over the long term, the income should rise to the level of $500, but we should not be afraid to start more modestly to get there. Given the glacial pace of change in Washington, we can also begin organizing in states to create smaller state-based income floors.

To be clear, I'm not proposing a universal basic income. Proponents of that idea favor giving every American, regardless of their wealth or whether they work, $1,000 a month with no strings attached at a cost of several trillion dollars. A guaranteed income for working people, by contrast, would go to a more narrow set of recipients, specifically working people in need, and it would cost much less.

The idea of a guaranteed income that encourages work isn't a fringe idea. Nearly a dozen Nobel Prize–winning economists believe that it's a smart way to grow the economy and reduce inequality. Many of them do not make their case from a moral perspective, but from a practical one. "The pie is growing bigger, there is no guarantee that everyone will benefit if we leave the market alone," explains Nobel laureate Sir Christopher Pissarides, a professor at the London School of Economics, whose words echo comments of other Nobel Prize winners. "A universal minimum income is one of those ways, in fact, it is one I am very much in favor of, as long as we know how to apply it without taking away incentive to work at the lower end of the market."

A guaranteed income designed in this particular way—$500 a month to working people making under $50,000—would be the most powerful tool we have to combat inequality in our country. And it would encourage work by making it pay.

6

WORTHWHILE WORK

My father worked as a traveling salesman at Snyder Paper Corporation for 39 years. On his last day on the job before he retired, his colleagues rented the ballroom at the Holiday Inn in our hometown of Hickory for a farewell lunch. I was in eighth grade at the time and I got to take the day off from school—a nearly unprecedented event in our family—to join the celebration.

My dad was visibly anxious as we walked into the hotel. He carried a leather-bound notebook in which he'd written his speech, and he kept passing it from one hand to the other while compulsively clearing his throat. His nerves were contagious. I felt butterflies in my own stomach as we passed a banner emblazoned with his name in big letters, congratulating him on his long run. Pacing back and forth between our small dining room and kitchen, he had rehearsed his speech for days, speaking with a formal, foreign-seeming diction, with little trace of his usual Southern lilt. This was one of the most important moments of his life, and he wanted to get it right.

That was 20 years ago, and I can't remember a thing he said when he finally stood at the podium. I do, however, remember his fellow salesmen, the managers in suits and ties, and the warehouse workers encircling him afterward, smiling broadly and laughing as they shook his hand and hugged him. He was the center of attention, and his community had come out to support him. For one hour of one afternoon, at the very end of his career, he got to be small-town royalty.

My father had always been a charmer. At work he was everyone's confidant, their trusted advisor, informal therapist, and professional ally. He was the first to know when a secretary was pregnant, if a boss was cheating on his wife, or if a customer had lost a loved one. He didn't collect his intel from gossip but from quiet confidences shared in office hallways. People knew they could trust him.

My dad's customers, the people who bought the industrial paper he was selling, were some of his closest friends. He took care of them by listening to their stories, celebrating their successes, and comforting them in the worst of times. They took care of him in return. When he was 50, an inner ear condition caused him to become completely deaf in one ear. Before his eardrum was removed, he would suffer debilitating attacks of dizziness, nausea, and vertigo that came on without warning. On multiple occasions, his customers literally caught him as he fell and watched over him until he recovered or my mother arrived to take him home.

The professional community my dad built might have been stronger than most, but the relationships we cultivate in our workplaces are often sources of deep fulfillment. The Harvard political scientist Robert Putnam, who chronicled the erosion of civic and political engagement over the second half of the twentieth century in his book *Bowling Alone,* believes that the one source of enduring community in many Americans' lives is around the watercooler at work.

"Professionals and blue collar workers alike are putting in long hours together, eating lunch and dinner together, traveling together, arriving early, and staying late," he writes. "People are divorcing more often, marrying later (if at all), and living alone in unprecedented numbers. Work is where the heart is, then, for so many solitary souls."

Every second Wednesday, my father's sales route required him to spend a night away so he could visit his customers in small, sleepy towns in the western Carolinas with names like Shelby, Cherryville, and Gaffney. On summer Wednesdays, my mom and I, both out of school and with time to spare, would pile into his blue Oldsmobile and join him. Those nights away from home were a welcome break for me, an excuse to do something out of the ordinary. I had to sit in the stifling heat of the car while my dad made his sales calls, but then I got to play in the pool at the Fairfield Inn in the evening and get snacks and sodas from the vending machine—paradise for an eight-year-old.

On one trip, it was too hot to wait in the car, so I accompanied my father into a small, industrial building somewhere in rural South Carolina. The room smelled of ink and musk, and fans circulated the dusty, stale air. I had a Game Boy in hand, but I was really listening to my dad's conversation with the customer, who was in his fifties and balding. He spoke with an unusually thick accent, making it difficult for me to understand everything he said. My dad and he exchanged seemingly endless lighthearted banter. Then, at the end of their conversation, they got serious while they pored over a white binder with my dad's company logo on top. A moment later, we ducked outside, and I remember feeling a cool breeze on my face. My happy anticipation of the AC of the car now in sight paled in comparison to how elated my father was. He swung my hand in his, laughing as we walked back to the car. He had made a big sale, and his joy was infectious.

I have no doubt that some of his happiness that day came from the financial reward it would bring him, but even then I knew that it wasn't just about the money. I could feel that my father had achieved something unexpected, something he felt he deserved, and he was relishing the sense of accomplishment. Still today, he can talk enthusiastically about the weights of industrial paper sizes, the kinds of paper that work on certain printers, and the variety of colors to choose from. He enjoyed the challenge of his work at least as much as the relationships he was able to build along the way.

While not every day was fantastic, and there were many setbacks and tense evenings at home, my father wanted to work. The same goes for my mother, who loved her job teaching. She retired a few years earlier than most people do, just shy of her sixtieth birthday. In her final years at the small high school where she taught math, she had grown increasingly beleaguered with the nonteaching duties the school required of her. School administrators expected her to be hall monitor, bus line supervisor, and occasional public safety officer in her own classroom, as well as a talented instructor of algebra, geometry, and precalculus. But she loved what she did, because she knew that every now and then, she shaped the trajectory of one of her students' lives. Some became teachers themselves; still others, engineers or architects. Even after retiring, she volunteered to tutor students who were struggling.

Once when I was nine or ten, a 20-something woman awkwardly approached our table at a "fish camp"—shorthand for a cheap, Southern seafood restaurant where the featured items on the menu are popcorn shrimp, fried flounder, and coleslaw. "Mrs. Hughes!" she said as she sidled up next to us. "I just wanted to let you know how much of a difference you made in my life. I never got a chance to tell you that, and I am just so grateful." My mom tilted her head to the side and gave a warm, toothy smile, nodding in appreciation and thanks. They chatted briefly, and a moment after the woman left, my mom turned back to my father and me and said sheepishly, "I have never seen that woman before in my life." She wasn't forgetful or insincere—it was just that she had taught thousands and thousands of students over the years. Even she couldn't keep track of the impact she had.

Most people in America, at least in this regard, are a lot like my parents. I've talked with historians, economists, scholars, cashiers, and gig economy workers about how technology is changing work and what people believe is core to who Americans are. There is one thing that both elite and ordinary people, on the left and the right, tend to agree on: people are better off when they work. They of course need to work to be able to afford the basics of a roof over their heads, food on the table, an education for their kids, and to see a doctor when they are sick. But people also want to work because it gives their lives meaning, community, and purpose. Every person deserves to feel a sense of reward from their work, just as much as they deserve a sense of financial security in their lives.

Normally, those who advocate for a guaranteed income do not talk a lot about work. If they do, many tend to see a guaranteed income as a way to prepare for a world without work, or at least a time when there will be a lot less of it. But I believe work is essential to who we are and who we want to be. Work that is rewarding and meaningful—including traditionally unpaid work like caregiving and getting an education—makes us happier, healthier, and more fulfilled. We know this intuitively, but psychological studies also show that people who work are happier, are healthier, and even live longer. By contrast, people who lack paid employment for long periods of time have a much higher rate of falling into depression, exhibiting symptoms like irritability, difficulty concentrating and making decisions, and insomnia. The unemployed also report higher rates of feeling like they are a disappointment to their families or to themselves. Having a new job can reverse those feelings over time, but it takes longer to recover from depression than it does to fall into it. The pain that comes from joblessness can be deep, enduring, and stubbornly persistent.

The stress and depression that accompany unemployment can have a very real and concrete impact on our bodies and even cause us to die earlier. Anne Case and Angus Deaton's recent shocking studies have drawn attention to the rising death rates among white Americans without high school degrees, some of the people who have been the most affected by changes in the labor market. Case and Deaton's work connects these "deaths of despair," as they call them, to the cumulative disadvantages that follow from low employment.

Higher rates of substance abuse and suicide are at fault for many of the negative health effects and early deaths that are correlated with unemployment. Unemployed people are more prone to alcohol and drug abuse and the kind of psychological struggles that lead people to early death by suicide. Someone who is unemployed is more than twice as likely to use illegal drugs than someone who is employed full time. The correlation between unemployment rates and opioid abuse in particular is staggering: for every 1 percent increase in the unemployment rate in a given county, the opioid death rate rises by nearly 4 percent, and emergency room visits rise by 7 percent.

While it is true that work seems to keep us healthier, sometimes we can take our obsession with work too far. Political leaders glorify the "dignity of work" and claim work of any sort is better than no work at all. Donald Trump and Joe Biden compete to see who can speak more for "Scranton values," grounding their arguments in the idea that even demeaning jobs are better than no jobs. Civil rights activists have historically voiced similar ideas. Martin Luther King Jr., in his speeches about labor, celebrated the dignity of work. "If a man is called to be a street sweeper," he said in 1967, "he should sweep streets even as a Michelangelo painted, or Beethoven composed music or Shakespeare wrote poetry. He should sweep streets so well that all the hosts of heaven and earth will pause to say, 'Here lived a great street sweeper who did his job well.'. . . No work is insignificant. All labor that uplifts humanity has dignity and importance and should be undertaken with painstaking excellence."

Even the smallest contributions to society are worthwhile, but it is also true that we should want more meaningful work that can't just be done by a machine. The problem with the glorification of the dignity of work is that it flattens the idea of work itself and makes no distinction between purposeful work, busywork, and work to destructive ends. Some work is meaningful and rewarding, and other work sheer drudgery. Some work is directed toward destructive ends—drug dealers and insider traders have strong work ethics, too. When we imbue the dignity of work with a kind of religious meaning, it obscures the fact that the kind of work we want more of is the kind that is purpose-driven and fulfilling: positive, substantive work that earns esteem.

Unfortunately, a lot of work in America today is draining and tedious. Retail and service sector jobs, the fastest-growing category of jobs in America, can involve standing over a fast-food cash register or deep fryer for hours on end. Backbreaking construction jobs require workers to toil outdoors in all seasons, including in the depths of winter.

Home and office cleaning jobs are some of the least rewarding and most physically punishing jobs out there, not to mention the lots of coal miners or slaughterhouse workers. While even bad jobs provide a sense of purpose to some, many are stuck in them because they are the only options they have to pay the bills.

The "dignity of work" phrase is often co-opted and used as a cynical tool, especially by people on the political right, to force people out of social welfare programs. Frances Fox Piven and Bruce Cloward documented in their landmark history *Regulating the Poor* the myriad ways that government has used arbitrary rules to inspect people's homes, to ban them from having color televisions, or to force women to answer extremely personal questions. An early version of welfare, called Aid for Families with Dependent Children (AFDC), may have seemed generous in spirit, but was invasive in practice. "AFDC mothers, for example, are often forced to answer questions about their sexual behavior ('When did you last menstruate?'), open their closets to inspection ('Whose pants are those?'), and permit their children to be interrogated ('Do any men visit your mother?')," Piven and Cloward wrote. "Unannounced raids, usually after midnight and without benefit of warrant, in which a recipient's home is searched for signs of 'immoral' activities, have also been part of life on AFDC." Work requirements follow in a long tradition of similar kinds of regulations organized to regulate the lives of the poor rather than actually encourage any kind of meaningful, rewarding work.

This continues today. For example, Arkansas' governor, Asa Hutchinson, has aggressively implemented work requirements across every major social safety net program in his state in order to reduce the number of people who qualify. He has kicked tens of thousands of people off of food stamps by proclaiming that if you can't find a job that employs you for 20 hours a week in Arkansas, you no longer qualify for any kind of nutritional assistance. (Even in a period of low unemployment, there are still tens of thousands of Arkansans who find themselves temporarily jobless in any given month, often through no fault of their own.) Several states are looking to follow suit, and Republicans are considering implementing a similar kind of requirement nationally. As if that's not enough, Hutchinson has requested a waiver from the federal government to implement the same policy for the 240,000 residents of his state who are too poor to afford health care and rely on Medicaid when they have emergencies. In the periods of life when they don't have a job, they will have no access to affordable health insurance. In Arkansas, "work requirements" is code for a strategy to make the lives of poor people more difficult.

Enforcement of these work requirements plays into dangerous racial stereotypes about who is benefiting from government assistance. The infamous "welfare queens" invoked by Ronald Reagan are a mythological figure in American consciousness with deep roots in racist stereotypes. The dignity of work is often used to invoke imagery of white men on assembly lines, demonstrating determination and resilience to provide for their families, in implied contrast to images of black women who passively rely on government handouts. Nothing could be further from the truth. In fact, labor force participation rates are higher for single black mothers (76 percent) than for white men (72 percent). And that doesn't even take into account any nontraditional work like caregiving that many women do.

The malicious ways work requirements have been used in the past make me suspicious of some calls on the left for a federal job guarantee in lieu of a guaranteed income. Its basic premise is that the tens of millions of people who aren't participating in the formal workforce can only be guaranteed economic security if they sign up for newly created, but still undefined, government jobs. One of the most concrete plans put forward by journalist Jeff Spross imagines that municipal government employees will hunt out local infrastructure projects and ask churches and civic organizations to submit ideas for new jobs. "People seeking jobs would come to these local offices, which would draw on the federal databases to link the potential workers up with the most appropriate projects," he writes. "Crucially, workers would be matched with nearby jobs according to skills they already have." The cost would be significantly higher than a guaranteed income, up to $775 billion a year for 14 million new government employees.

There is little evidence that such a job guarantee program would work. A 2015 study by prominent economists ranked the effectiveness of 200 examples of labor market interventions. They found that subsidized public-sector employment programs consistently came in last, sometimes even having negative impacts. The arguments for a federal job guarantee require faith in government's ability to connect people to jobs they want and need. The idea of relying on a DMV-like federal jobs database to help local nonprofits and churches match 14 million people up with new jobs seems far-fetched at best. Government can and already does provide good public service jobs to lots of people—nearly 15 percent of the American workforce is already employed by federal, state, or local governments. But relying on a job guarantee to provide broad economic stability is a step too far. It falls squarely in the tradition of government telling poor and middle-class people what to do with their lives, dictating what counts as a real job and what doesn't.

What we need instead is a social policy that provides people with opportunities to find the kinds of fulfilling work they want and deserve. The best way to guarantee that is to empower people with cash to secure extra training, pay for childcare, or move to a place with more opportunities. As we will see later, evidence from existing American programs shows that a little bit of cash doesn't cause people to drop out of the workforce, but instead helps them find work. If people have financial stability from a guaranteed income, they can choose work that's fulfilling, purpose-driven, and a match for their skills.

Today, a Walmart worker who suffers from harassment in the workplace or extreme scheduling demands receives no unemployment insurance if she quits. With a guaranteed income in the background, she wouldn't be able to drop out of the workforce altogether, but she would have a small cushion to help make ends meet for a few months while she looked for a new job. (Because her tax return showed she worked last year, she'd receive the guaranteed income for the entirety of this year.) That kind of security would also allow her to turn down a dead-end job, even if it paid a little more than one that might grow into something better in time.

For some people, the most fulfilling and rewarding work may not be paid at all. This uncompensated work plays an important role in our society, and we should recognize it as the real work it is. In our modern technical language, people are said to be working only if they have formal paid employment from a legally recognized business entity: they receive W-4 or 1099 forms, their salaries are regulated by minimum wage laws, and their productivity is counted as a part of economic statistics like GDP.

But historically, these lines were not so brightly drawn. On the farm my grandfather grew up on, everyone was expected to pitch in to grow crops, keep house, and take care of one another. We wouldn't recognize much of this activity today as work, even though it clearly was. Our current definition of work is a relatively recent invention that emerged as people moved off family farms and into employment relationships that could be codified and made visible to the state. Work became narrowly defined—and tended to line up with the activities of white men.

But a parent who stays at home today, takes care of young children, cooks, cleans, and runs errands is no less productive than a factory worker or an entrepreneur. An adult who takes care of an aging loved one—dressing, feeding, and bathing Mom or Dad—has full days of exhausting, socially valuable activity. Students who spend hours and hours a week sitting in classrooms, studying at night, writing papers, and preparing for tests are also working, just not for pay. As long as you're doing something for your community, we should recognize you as a worker. This would be a bigger and more modern definition of work than what we have used for the past few decades and more in line with the long-term historical view of what work really is.

Thirty million Americans participate in this unrecognized workforce and are barred from many of the government benefits tied to work, causing many of them to live at or near the poverty line. According to the American Enterprise Institute, a conservative think tank, a quarter of the people who live in poverty do not work in paid jobs because childcare or eldercare would cost more than they would earn. Another fifth of the unemployed people who are below the poverty line are in school. In other words, nearly half of the "nonworking" poor are working to provide care for their families or to improve themselves through education.

All of these examples—childcare, eldercare, and higher education—are already visible on the tax returns that Americans file. We claim dependents and report the tuition that we pay. We do not need to create any new bureaucracy to verify the claims, because they are audited by the Internal Revenue Service each year. A more expansive definition of work should also include community and religious service and artistic work, although these are harder to verify. Over the long term, we should determine how to verify if people are involved in these activities in order to include them in this broader definition of work. But we can start today by including caregiving and education in how we shape our social policy. That way we can begin to recognize the contributions that tens of millions of people in alternative work arrangements are making for their families and communities.

Perhaps counterintuitively, many of these jobs are the jobs of the future. Caregiving in particular is an area of massive job growth. Our country's fastest-growing demographic is people over age 85, and by 2050, the total number of elderly in need of personal care will number 27 million, more than double the number today. Many people are naturally distrustful of the institutions that house the elderly, seemingly for good reason. The majority of people who end up in nursing homes die within two years, even though nearly half of Medicaid's entire budget funds the exorbitant fees they require. Many Americans would prefer to take care of their aging loved ones at home, and it seems that it might help them live longer and lower the costs of care.

But the people who take on care and housing responsibilities directly pay a steep personal cost. "Seventy percent of caregivers report making changes such as cutting back on their working hours, changing jobs, stopping work entirely, taking a leave of absence, or other such changes as a result of their caregiving role," scholar and organizer Ai-Jen Poo notes in her book *The Age of Dignity.* The amount of income caregivers forfeit is staggering—more than $300,000 per person over the course of a lifetime, according to the AARP. "Often they do this without support for, or even acknowledgment of, the extra work, which diminishes their ability to be present and productive in other arenas of life."

Our aging parents and grandparents will increasingly need caregiving at home, but our current policies do not recognize this as work. Nor do they recognize the work of the tens of millions of parents of children under the age of five, who demand constant attention from a parent or other relative. Mothers in particular spend enormous amounts of time feeding, washing, cleaning, and cooking, but have never had their work recognized for what it is.

A small group of economists has strived over decades to precisely quantify the value of work that goes uncounted in domestic activities like childcare and eldercare, food preparation, cleaning, and home maintenance. By using the American Time Use Survey, a widely trusted method for quantifying the amount of time Americans spend on different activities, they estimate that America's GDP would be a full 26 percent higher if we counted domestic labor as work.

That means that over $4 trillion of economic activity is going unrecognized because of our outdated definitions of who is working—not to mention the fact that these workers don't get paid. Historically, the people who do this unrecognized work are disproportionately women and people of color, groups that the law has consistently neglected.

Even these numbers do not recognize the work of the millions of students enrolled in American universities. Students are not paid for their time, because the effort they invest today will pay off in future years. But every student deserves to have basic financial stability to enable them to focus on their studies and help supplement the cost of food or childcare. Wealthy students have the advantage of a kind of "guaranteed income" from parents who want to do everything possible to keep them focused on their studies. Poor and middle-class students deserve the same.

In an ideal world, every person should have the chance to do work they love. The satisfaction my parents got from their jobs showed me at a young age what's possible when you love your work. The opportunity to advocate for a guaranteed income in my day-to-day work is one of the most fulfilling parts of my life. A few hundred extra dollars a month isn't going to mean everyone gets to have the job they want overnight, but it is the kind of boost that a person can use to invest in vocational school or to move closer to a job they think fits their skills best. It can be a universal strike fund, which enables someone to quit a job with an abusive manager. It can allow a person to reduce their hours to make more time at home to take care of a young child or aging parent. It can be the seed money to start a small business around the corner or on Etsy. A guaranteed income would give millions more people a little more of a chance to choose the work that is right for them.

A small number of people who are unable to work, particularly the infirm, disabled, or geographically isolated, may be left behind by a guaranteed income tied to a broad definition of work. These people deserve support as well, and programs like Social Security Disability Insurance provide a critical safety net to support them. My uncle suffered from degenerating discs in his spine in his forties, the result of decades of pulling cables in a physically demanding workplace. He had been injured as a child when a tractor ran over him on the family farm, and the workplace injuries compounded the original damage, rendering him disabled for life. Without Social Security disability payments, he never would have been able to support himself or my aunt as he has in the decades since.

This is what the safety net is for—to help those who can't work. For everyone else who is working in traditional or untraditional jobs but still can't make ends meet, a guaranteed income is the most efficient way to ensure that they have stability and a chance to find work that's fulfilling and matches their skills. People want to work. Let's make sure it pays for them to do so.

7

UNTETHERED
IDEALISM

I arrived at O'Hare International Airport in February 2007, carrying a backpack stuffed with a laptop and a half-dozen books and dragging an oversized roll-aboard suitcase behind me. I had come to Chicago in the midst of one of its worst winters in memory to work for Barack Obama's presidential campaign. My now husband and I had packed up all our possessions in Palo Alto and put them in storage purgatory until we found a new apartment. I hopped on the Blue Line and headed straight for Obama's temporary campaign offices on the seventeenth floor of a skyscraper in the Loop.

Facebook's growing popularity—it was up to almost 18 million users—mattered little to the operatives who were setting up shop in Chicago. Eventually the campaign manager, David Plouffe, greeted me, thanked me for being there, and promptly turned his attention back to whatever it was he had been working on. My new boss, Joe Rospars, wasn't in the office that day, but he had warned me to quash any talk of Obama as the Facebook candidate. "It's going to take an extra effort from you to make clear that you're taking a leave from Facebook to work as an organizer here, and more importantly that this campaign and its energy are not about Facebook at all," he wrote in an e-mail before I arrived.

I found my way to the sole digital person in the office. Jon Jones was roughly my age and already looked a little haggard and unshaven, even though the campaign had just begun. He and I immediately clicked. He was from Scranton, Pennsylvania, the son of working-class parents who had done everything in their power to make it possible for him to go to Tufts. Like me, he joined the campaign for the most idealistic of reasons: he was inspired by Barack Obama's story and pragmatic idealism. While the rest of the political world thought we were crazy for backing an African American freshman senator with the middle name Hussein, we thought he was a change candidate who had a real shot at upending the Democratic primary, and maybe even winning the White House. All the staffers who took risks to join that campaign in the early days believed that the unexpected could become real.

Those first couple weeks in Chicago were a blur. I found an apartment, started hiring a team, and got to work alongside Jon on a variety of tasks: cutting videos of rallies, setting up landing pages where people could RSVP to future events, editing mass e-mails for clarity and voice, and, inevitably, curating the senator's Facebook and MySpace pages. One day bled into the next, each busier and more frantic than the last. As our digital team grew, we managed to build a social network of nearly a million members, a platform for supporters to organize groups, host grassroots events, and set their own fund-raising goals.

I didn't find the technical work of building and managing the network to be nearly as much of a challenge as the human dimension of organizing people. I had to provide activists with enough guidance to help them understand what the campaign needed from them, but not so much that they felt like we were narrowly instructing them on what to think and do. Even more challenging, we had to convince the campaign's senior management to let go of the typical top-down command-and-control structure, in which headquarters dictates the message and micromanages field operations, and instead embrace a decentralized approach that enabled supporters to self-organize digitally. It seems small in retrospect, but the idea of allowing any supporter, no matter how passionate or unhinged, to write anything they liked on a blog on a campaign website—or to organize events, even if they had no training—was unprecedented. The more freedom we gave supporters, coupled with guidance on what the campaign needed, the stronger the network grew. We were initially the crazy tech guys in the corner, but as the number of dollars donated and volunteers recruited through the platform grew, it was clear we were onto something. Over time we earned more autonomy, and I was able to recruit a team of nearly a dozen people focused exclusively on helping volunteers organize through the campaign's social network.

Before we hit send on our victory e-mail and text messages on election night, reporters and academics were already writing articles and reports about how we did it. A lot of them paid attention to the idiosyncrasies of the technology we had developed, but our victory didn't happen because of any flashy features—most of that was off-the-shelf and pretty straightforward. It happened because we were able to convince the people running a traditionally hier-archical institution to work with a different kind of grass-roots, digital structure. Activists and volunteers could feel the difference, and they were invigorated by the power we placed in their hands.

Facebook and the Obama campaign, the first two ca-reer experiences of my life, both taught me a clear lesson: to aim high and expect the unexpected. Change could happen nearly overnight with the right team and values. Those ex-periences gave me faith in my ability to buck tradition and to update institutions for a new digital era.

When I decided a couple years later to do something similarly unlikely—find a new business model for tradi-tional print media—a lot of people, including myself, thought that it just might be possible. One major success could be a fluke, but two was indicative of some kind of gift, people told me. When rumors began circulating that I was looking to buy *The New Republic* magazine, a 100-year-old institution of the intellectual left, the *Huffington Post* made it their big, banner story for a day, with the headline "SAVIOR OF THE REPUBLIC?"

That headline was so ridiculous, and my blind ambition so irrationally bold, that any cool-headed outsider could have seen how the story would end. What went wrong at *The New Republic* has a direct bearing on my work today. It is the driving reason why I favor a more modest guaran-teed income over the universal basic income (UBI) idea that has become increasingly popular over the past two years. I learned how counterproductive unbridled idealism can be if it lacks practical grounding in the here and now.

A few months before I decided to buy the magazine, I went to the basement of the New York Public Library to comb through old issues. The only way I could see and read the earliest ones was to request physical reels from the librarian and fire up a 1970s-vintage microfiche machine that I could hardly believe still functioned. I spun through the issues, reel after reel, year after year, over the course of two or three days. I would roll forward and stop at a random moment and then read through all of the articles on the page. It was a rapid education in the changing sensibilities of the magazine and how much it had driven ideas in liberal politics over the course of the twentieth century.

I had read *The New Republic* off and on, mostly online, since college, but I did not have a deep appreciation for the historical moment that it was born into in 1914, or for the values of its founding editors. It had been acerbic and contrarian in its recent past, publishing shameful articles like Charles Murray's "The Bell Curve" and cheerleading George W. Bush's decision to invade Iraq. But for most of its history, I came to understand, it was more in line with values I shared. Confidently liberal and market-oriented, it pressed the need for a strong central government to guarantee the rights and freedoms that the Progressive Era—from which it had emerged—had fought for.

For me, *The New Republic* was more an institution of American intellectual life than a physical print magazine.

It addressed both the political questions of the day and the concerns of literature, philosophy, and culture. What if we could bring the power of its journalism to new, bigger audiences both in print and on the screens people carried everywhere? We could invest in both print and digital in tandem, without sacrificing one for the other.

In the late fall of 2011, I reached out to the owners, a collection of Wall Street investors led by Bill Ackman and Larry Grafstein, who had recently put the magazine on the market. They were surprised that someone with a largely digital background would be interested in a magazine with a circulation of less than 40,000 losing millions of dollars a year. Although I didn't know it at the time, I was the only potential bidder with any real interest. I officially purchased the magazine in March 2012 and headed down to Washington to speak with its staff.

Franklin Foer, who had edited *The New Republic* for a number of years earlier but was now an editor-at-large (a mostly symbolic title on the masthead), showed up at that first meeting and sat in the back of the room. I ran into him in the hallway afterward, and we connected immediately. Over the next few months, Frank and I met several times to discuss his previous tenure at *The New Republic* and our shared belief in the power of narrative journalism to shape the dialogue of the country. I liked that he had years of experience already in the editor role but I could see that he might bring a fresh creative energy to the work. The D.C.-born son of an antitrust lawyer, Frank was naturally suspicious of the concentration of power in the hands of elites, yet he also called many powerful people friends. His knowledge and experience were wide-ranging and he exuded a winning charm. I made him an offer, and he began his second stint as editor early that summer.

Our first order of business was to invest. The magazine had been on a shoestring budget for years, and we believed the lack of investment was the primary thing holding it back. We offered eye-popping sums to bring on new talented journalists and to retain the best we had. We created a deep bench of senior editors who were some of the most talented journalists in Washington. We tried to appeal to a broader audience by publishing cover stories on Chris Christie's shady backroom deals and the epidemic of unregulated day care centers alongside reviews of television's *Girls* and critiques of Ai Weiwei's "terrible" art.

Frank and I wanted to bring new life to the digital and print pages of the publication. We envisioned a magazine and a website that were at once classy and vibrant, highbrow and accessible. In redesigning the print edition, we tried to meld the look and feel of old literary journals, like *The Partisan Review* from the 1950s, with the splashy contemporary style of *New York* magazine. To accomplish this, we hired *The New Republic*'s first full-time art director, an award-winning designer from *Newsweek*, and a team of print designers who were qualified to work at institutions several times our size. We invested in engineering and website development alongside our traditional direct mail program. These investments took *The New Republic*'s annual losses from around $2 million a year up to $6 million nearly overnight.

Everyone on the outside assumed I intended to transform *The New Republic* into a personal megaphone, or at the very least to use it to advance my own political agenda. But over four years, I wrote only one piece for the website, on the rise of big data, and a short note reflecting on Jeff Bezos's purchase of *The Washington Post*. The journalists and academics who wrote for us were some of the smartest, most sophisticated minds in media, and whatever I happened to think about the Iraqi surge or Mitt Romney's tax policies felt superficial in comparison. Close friends marveled at how much I talked about the business side of things and how little I had to say about what Frank was planning to put on the cover.

Instead, I became obsessed with how to turn the numbers in our financial statements from red to black. I had no interest in making a profit from *The New Republic*, but I did want to make it resilient and sustainable. I believed a break-even business would be a testament to the strength of the publication and an indicator of the value of our journalism. This became a personal challenge for me, a kind of Golden Fleece that I woke up each morning in pursuit of. Making the business work was about something much bigger than the numbers on the P&L: it was about attaining an idealistic, nearly impossible goal, just like we had at Facebook and in the Obama campaign. I wanted to be the one who "figured out" the model that took aging jewels of print journalism and set them on a surer path in a digital world.

I worked at a frenzied pace, learning the nitty-gritty of sales and business management. I traveled to Chicago, San Francisco, Washington, and other cities to sell junior ad buyers on our small-circulation scholarly political magazine. A year in, I found myself in a nondescript building on the outskirts of Detroit. Across from me, a 22-year-old ad buyer at a media agency chewed gum while she told us she had never heard of *The New Yorker,* let alone *The New Republic.* She flipped through our magazine rapidly, as if she were looking for the photographs of Jennifer Aniston that she'd find in *US Weekly.* The idea that I could ever convince her to buy a page in *The New Republic* was absurd, but my belief that I could do the impossible made me grit my teeth and push my way through. I didn't leave that meeting feeling deflated—I left angry and more determined than ever to create a world where our star would rise so convincingly that even she would have to say yes the next time I called on her.

Two and a half years went by. The writing that filled our pages was beautiful and at times impactful. Our web traffic picked up lightly and even our print subscriptions rose by a bit. Our editorial staff told Frank and me that they felt happy and satisfied with our direction. Meanwhile, I was becoming more desperate. We had signed up a small set of new advertisers, but they paid much less than anyone had predicted. I had bet that *The New Republic*'s prestige and elite audience would command a higher premium, but after years of trying I learned that few advertisers were willing to pay to be in a small, somewhat partisan magazine, regardless of the quality of its iPad app, journalism, or design. We were losing just as much money as before because our business endeavors weren't showing a trace of traction. I lost sleep over the design of our subscription page and the marginal effectiveness of a direct mail campaign to gain more subscribers. I spent hours in meetings trying to optimize our pages for Google search results, missing the forest for the trees.

We had tried our hand at events, apparel, and video, with some success, but it was clear none of these was going to right the ship. The fundamental math of the business just didn't work. The market of subscribers and advertisers was too small to bridge the huge financial chasm that we had dug for ourselves with our early investments. I was writing checks for $500,000 every month to cover our losses, and each one felt like a private confession that I did not have the financial and management skills that I thought I had years earlier. I needed help.

The only option I hadn't tried was bringing in executive leadership and investing that person with the authority to run the company day to day. The owner of *The Atlantic,* David Bradley, had lost tens of millions of dollars for years, until he brought in a seasoned media executive. Within a couple of years, the *Atlantic*'s new CEO brought the company close to break even, buoyed by a strong events program and a heavy emphasis on increasing digital traffic by writing pithy, timely updates for a broader audience to accompany *The Atlantic*'s long-form journalism. It seemed clear, at least to me, that our pristine and cultured website would have to begin courting mass appeal, while at the same time continuing the highbrow analysis *The New Republic* was synonymous with. In the late summer of 2014, I retained a recruiting firm to begin a search for a CEO.

I interviewed dozens of candidates, and Frank spent time with the final three. I chose Guy Vidra, a 40-something executive at Yahoo who had turned around businesses of our size. Guy's vision was clear: a new, firmer emphasis on traffic metrics, a slimmer editorial staff, more talk of content partnerships, and more experimentation with video. The editorial team had little enthusiasm for his approach. They felt like it was a zero-sum game: an emphasis on digital traffic would come at the expense of quality long-form. I hoped that we'd be able to reconcile differences through a collective commitment to making a popular and sustainable *New Republic,* but unfortunately that was not to be the case.

Guy and Frank clashed continually over the fall, and Guy recommended that we bring in new editorial leadership. I backed his decision even though I had meaningful reservations. If I was going to hold Guy accountable for the success of the business, I had to empower him to work with a leadership team he trusted. Guy began quietly interviewing candidates for a new editor, and word got back to Frank.

Frank resigned in an impromptu speech to the newsroom and then hosted a gathering for all the Washington staff at his home that evening. The following morning, a dozen senior staffers resigned en masse, and most of the freelance contributing editors asked to have their names removed from the masthead as well. We were left with nine editorial staffers, a fraction of the powerhouse roster that had showed up for work just the day before.

The public narrative quickly became a story of principled journalists standing up to the corrosive forces of Silicon Valley. The decision the editorial staff had made to walk out on the institution that they claimed to care so much about made little sense to me. In retrospect I can understand how my bringing in a digital media executive felt like a betrayal of what I had been consistently saying for years. I mistakenly presumed that they would know I harbored no secret desire to turn *The New Republic* into the next *BuzzFeed*. Instead, many of the editors accused me of harboring motivations that were insidious and malevolent. One former senior editor, Julia Ioffe, made a tour of media outlets to claim that I was "downright contemptuous and hostile" to the staff. I felt the editors unfairly painted me as a destructive force and a dumb princeling, King Joffrey in the flesh, even though they knew that was not who I was.

In hindsight, my decision to hold on to the dream of a break-even *New Republic* was a mistake. I should have accepted that the future model for institutions like *The New Republic* is likely to be the same as the one from its past: to rely on generous benefactors to cover moderate losses year to year. *The New Republic* had been bought and sold a dozen times in its 100-year history, but it was really a cause dressed up as a company. It was a nonprofit that always had, and always would, serve a small, cultivated audience. We might sweep a few million people into our net in any given month online, but the number of dedicated readers who cared would never be more than 100,000. The sustainable "business" solution I sought was achievable through largesse and through largesse alone.

Washington closed ranks, and the country club that I had effectively joined when I bought the magazine firmly and decisively expelled me. Dinner invitations were rescinded. Friends took to Twitter to publicly renounce their relationships with me. A year later, a person I had never met before greeted me politely at a holiday party at the home of the ambassador to the United Nations. He asked me how I was, and then raised his voice in a scream: "Shame! Shame on you for what you did to those people!" Half of the people in the room turned their heads to look. He and others like him saw me as the crusader from Silicon Valley intent on destroying the civic traditions of the Fourth Estate. I had fired a beloved magazine editor in a time of deep anxiety about the future of journalism, and in doing so, had touched a nerve that ran deeper than I could have ever imagined.

After the editorial staff left, I spent another year with a new team, trying to reinvigorate the company. Despite their valiant efforts, we saw little progress. Eventually I learned what everyone else had known the whole time: *The New Republic* would never break even. Unless I had a political agenda to promote or an axe to grind, and a belief that absorbing millions in losses each year was the best way to do it, there was no future in my ownership. I decided to sell and a few months later, four years almost to the day that I bought it, I walked out of *The New Republic*'s office for the last time.

Looking back, there is no question I should have made space for a more measured idealism. The grand plans I came to the magazine with ironically caused me to go too far, too fast, undermining the institution I wanted to shore up and strengthen. Had I spent the $25 million I invested over those four years differently, it would have been enough to underwrite more modest ambitions for the institution for a decade or more.

In my work today I purposefully choose more modest means to accomplish otherwise idealistic and ambitious goals.

As with *The New Republic* and the Obama campaign, I was initially drawn to the idea of a guaranteed income because of the big-picture ideals. I loved the grandiosity of the idea—a world with no poverty, where everyone has a solid financial foundation to follow their dreams. I loved that it put the reins of responsibility in the hands of recipients, respecting their dignity to make their own decisions about where they wanted to live and what they wanted to spend their money on. Research showed that people with a guaranteed income would make better decisions as a result of living at least one step back from the threshold of financial catastrophe. The decentralized, market-driven nature of the benefit would create little new bureaucracy, making it one of the most efficient anti-poverty interventions out there.

Martin Luther King Jr.'s writing on the guaranteed income made a particularly deep impression on me, and over time I returned to his words again and again, almost as if they were scripture. I scoured collections of his sermons and speeches to trace the evolution of his thinking, and found some of the most inspiring words on the topic ever written. "The dignity of the individual," he wrote in his final book, "will flourish when the decisions concerning his life are in his own hands, when he has the assurance that his income is stable and certain, and when he knows that he has the means to seek self-improvement."

King put the emphasis on dignity. Other activists and thinkers on the left and right have made the case that without financial security, no one can be truly free. Belgian philosopher Philippe Van Parijs has been one of the most visible and ardent advocates for the idea that we cannot imagine a society with true freedom unless all its members have the ability to invest in themselves and make their own autonomous decisions. Friedrich Hayek and Milton Friedman made a similar case. Many of these twentieth-century thinkers followed in the tradition of writers like Thomas Paine and Thomas More. For centuries, philosophers have argued that only a guaranteed income can grant every individual the freedom that civilization is meant to provide.

I knew from my own extreme example that liberation from economic scarcity dramatically expands a person's freedom and enables them to figure out what they want and who they want to be. That first $100,000 windfall bonus I made at age 22 from Facebook effectively gave me a guaranteed income of $5,000 a year for life, assuming a 5 percent annual rate of return that many investors plan on. That would never have been enough to cover all my expenses, but being able to count on that much income enabled me to feel like I had a little more security. The further you get from subsistence, the easier it is to ask fundamental questions like: What do I want, and how do I get it? What are my values, and what will I use this money to invest in? A guaranteed income would acknowledge and empower the agency that exists inside every human being—the ability to create his or her own future.

In the early days of my work on the issue I found the purity of the ideals behind a guaranteed income intoxicating and wildly exciting. Later on I would learn more about the large body of evidence that undergirds the practical case for the effectiveness of cash transfers, but at the start, the boldness and idealism of an income floor for all was what drove me. But I also knew to be wary of untethered idealism. As I began exploring the feasibility of a guaranteed income, I kept thinking about what I learned from *The New Republic*:

just because an idea is bold does not mean that the means to achieve it need to be. A prosaic and incremental approach can be a more effective way to put poetic ideals into practice.

I found a collaborator with a similar disposition in Natalie Foster, an organizer and activist with a deep understanding of the changing nature of work. We had met socially years before, and she and I had both worked on President Obama's digital team at different times. We reconnected in January of 2016. I immediately loved her style. Direct, honest, and optimistic, she carried copies of a book on the basic income by Peter Barnes (*With Liberty and Dividends for All*) in her backpack and handed them out to anyone curious about the idea. Natalie was already beginning work to explore whether it might be feasible to start a guaranteed income at a city level, like in San Francisco.

Later that spring, I also met Dorian Warren, an academic and activist interested in exploring how a guaranteed income could contribute to the movement for racial justice. That year, in the midst of exploring the idea in policy papers, he wrote a call for a guaranteed income into the platform of the Movement for Black Lives. In May, Natalie, Dorian, and I traveled to Switzerland to better understand the dynamics at play in its nationwide referendum on the idea of a basic income. (The initiative failed, but the vote sparked a Europe-wide debate on the idea that continues today.)

The three of us shared a passion for building a world in which everyone has basic financial security. We also shared a fundamental caution: we wanted to better understand the issues and stakeholders involved before making any sweeping statements or big investments. We chose not to start a big campaign or even a new nonprofit, but instead organized a network of leaders into an initiative called the Economic Security Project to foster a deeper conversation around how a basic income might work. Over the past two years, we have convened leading thinkers across the country to talk about the guaranteed income in a range of settings, from big conferences to small dinners. Our team has joined community meetings and convened conversations in homeless shelters. We've raised money from a broad group of donors and invested millions of dollars in researchers, organizers, and artists to explore the idea of how a guaranteed income might work in practice, with the hope of inspiring more people to get involved in the work.

Importantly for all three of us, we did not start with a big proclamation for a UBI. Many people in our network found the initial language on our website tepid and too nuanced: "We believe people need financial security, and cash might be the most effective and efficient way to provide it" was in big, bold letters up top. The words "universal basic income" were buried further down the page, not because of a lack of passion for the ideals behind it, but because we purposefully wanted to go slow and create as much common ground as possible rather than setting unreasonably thin, ambitious goals too early.

We also knew from personal experience that the idea of a guaranteed income was not that clear. Despite its simplicity, most of the people I talked to who were not economists or philosophers would knit their eyebrows in confusion when I attempted to explain it. Each time I told someone—an old acquaintance, a taxi driver, the person next to me on a flight—what I was working on, confusion reigned. "Who gets money for nothing?" "It's not in exchange for something?" "How much money will people get, and how often?" "And who is paying for this?!" (That one often had the immediate follow-up, "Hopefully not me!") Most people would walk away curious at best, suspicious at worst.

In search of a more practical, less highfalutin way of talking about the idea, we turned our attention to the one place in America that already has a guaranteed income, albeit a small one: the state of Alaska. Each year every Alaskan gets about $1,400, or $120 a month, paid out of the Alaska Permanent Fund. The father of the fund was a man who governed in prose, not poetry. Jay Hammond, the Republican governor of Alaska from 1974 to 1982, had in his lifetime been a World War II fighter pilot, backcountry guide, and commercial fisherman. In the mid-1970s, during the heady days of the oil rush, Hammond found himself at the helm of a state flush with cash. He decided to propose a novel idea he had come up with years before when he was mayor of Bristol Bay Borough, a region of fishing villages in southwest Alaska with a tiny population. Hammond had noticed that the out-of-state companies that extracted millions of dollars of profit from commercial fishing were investing little to no money in the poor villages that their workers lived in. He proposed levying a 3 percent tax on fish and distributing the proceeds as a dividend to local residents. That plan was defeated, but just a few years later, he was significantly more successful in applying the same principle to a much more valuable natural resource: oil.

The Alaska Permanent Fund, conceived by Hammond and approved by a 2–1 margin in a 1976 referendum, deposits a quarter of the annual royalties from the production of oil and gas into a government-run savings account. Over the past 40 years, the fund has grown significantly: it is now worth $60 billion. Each year, 2.5 percent of the fund is divided up evenly among all of the residents, adults and children, of the state. Each person gets between $1,000 and $3,000 depending on the fund's earnings in the past few years, but the average amount is about $1,400. This means that in most years a family of four receives a check for a little less than $6,000 in October. A 2016 report from the University of Alaska's Institute of Social and Economic Research estimates that the dividend lifts 15,000 to 25,000 people above the poverty line, reducing the state's poverty rate by 25 percent while providing additional economic security to middle-class families.

To be clear, a hundred dollars a month is far from the guaranteed income that most idealists and philosophers imagine, but it is an income floor and the money comes like clockwork. The Economic Security Project, the group

Natalie, Dorian, and I started, commissioned empirical research to get hard numbers on what people did with the money and how they felt about it. We also talked with ordinary Alaskans in public forums, private one-on-one conversations, and anonymous focus groups. I heard many stories about how people felt about the dividend, and at first I was disappointed that Alaskans weren't saying that it was transformative and life-changing. They clearly cared about receiving the money—quantitative polling showed that more than 80 percent believed it was important to preserve the dividend and that the money was generally used well—but no one dressed the fund up in grand ideals. The phrase Alaskans did repeat was, "It helps me make ends meet." The dividend check reliably helps poor and middle-class families alike put away an extra month's worth of rent, pay down credit card debt, or buy holiday gifts. The words *freedom* and *dignity* didn't come up once. The dividend check did a simple and important thing: it helped them pay the bills.

As our work expanded and we had more conversations across America, we found again and again that the way most people think about money, work, and the challenge of making ends meet has little in common with the vocabulary of philosophers arguing for a basic income. People from every income and educational level, with all kinds of political beliefs and backgrounds, struggled to make sense of why anyone would support something like a basic income. The idea of money provided from nowhere and with no strings attached seemed nonsensical. Money always comes from somewhere—work, a gift, a loan, Social Security, an inheritance. Philosophers might think about money on a theoretical plane as an object of empowerment, but money only makes sense in practice in the concrete context of where it comes from and how it is used. A dollar found on the street is different than a dollar loaned from a family member, and that dollar is still different than one earned through work. One working-class woman in Detroit put it plainly: "I just don't understand where this money is coming from and why I would be getting it." Talking about money as an abstraction is something that seems to come from a place of privilege.

Looking back on my own childhood, we never talked about the money we had as "freeing" or as a source of dignity. Of course the middle-class salaries my parents made provided us with stability and a measure of autonomy, but the lived experience was much more prosaic. Money matters involved long, tedious Sunday afternoons, watching my parents peck away at the calculator, with bills spread out across the dining room table. It was the ledger of the checkbook that my mom taught me how to balance and forced me to use for my own accounting when I was ten years old. It was the $200 my parents allowed themselves to pull out of the bank each week for groceries, gas, and the occasional meal out. It was the coupons my mom clipped and saved in a pouch in her purse for our Friday afternoon grocery store trips.

Coupons, checkbooks, ATMs, and calculators were our day-to-day experience of money, but perhaps the most welcome kind of money was the tax rebate check my parents occasionally got from Uncle Sam. One thing that everyone on the left and right loves is a rebate check in the mail from the government. I still remember the $600 I got in 2008 from George Bush's attempt to stabilize the economy before the recession. The program was too little and too late to prevent the ensuing collapse, but the check was memorable. It arrived in a nondescript envelope but was a rainbow of colors and embossed with holograms, just like the ones my grandparents got from Social Security.

Similar checks come to many American households each year in the form of tax refunds, but few people know that a lot of the money in rebate checks is paid for by an anti-poverty program called the Earned Income Tax Credit, or the EITC. America almost established a guaranteed income fifty years ago, but created the EITC instead. It is a complicated-sounding benefit and an awkward acronym, but boring methods can sometimes accomplish big-picture ideals. The EITC is the framework we should use to make good on the promise of a guaranteed income for all working Americans.

8

EVERYBODY LIKES A TAX CREDIT

When I wasn't working on Facebook in college, I majored in history and literature. I was the kid who loved to speculate about things like Napoleon's thoughts after Waterloo or how James Baldwin felt when the publisher of *Giovanni's Room* told him to "burn" the manuscript. History wasn't just interesting to me: I came to understand that a better grasp of it could help us navigate the world we live in today. Lessons from the last American guaranteed income debate might inspire a new generation of activists and teach us how to most effectively wage the fight ahead. As Mark Twain allegedly said, "History doesn't repeat itself, but it often rhymes."

We got very close to creating an income floor in the United States once before. A little over 50 years ago, a Republican president proposed a guaranteed income, and the bill passed the House of Representatives. It failed in the Senate, but the framework for today's guaranteed income—the Earned Income Tax Credit—emerged from the ashes.

The 1960s chapter of the guaranteed income story doesn't start with the flower power of organized hippies, but with a set of conservative policymakers led by the Nobel Prize–winning economist Milton Friedman. Like many things in history, before him there was a woman who hatched the original idea who doesn't always get her due. In the 1940s in Britain, Lady Juliet Rhys-Williams developed the idea of the "negative income tax," which became the most popular design for how to create a guaranteed income for most of the twentieth century. She proposed a cash allowance delivered through the tax system. The more money a person makes, the higher the income tax they pay. So too, she argued, should a cash allowance increase the further below the poverty line a person falls. If the poverty line was set at £500, for example, and the negative tax rate was 50 percent, then a person who earned zero income would receive 50 percent of the poverty threshold, a guaranteed income of £250. If the person earned £200, then he would receive half of the difference between his wages and the poverty threshold, or £150, for a total income of £350. Once his wages passed the poverty line, he would begin paying taxes.

If you're confused, you're not alone. Most policymakers found the idea elegant in theory, but woefully difficult to understand. But for all its complexity, they loved that it would ensure that it paid to work. Recipients would always make more money from paid employment and benefits combined than they could from benefits alone.

The idea hopped the Atlantic, and American conservative economist Milton Friedman became a devoted advocate of it. Many conservatives of the time joined him in the belief that the negative income tax would be more efficient at helping people in poverty than the same amount of money invested in social services. "The advantages of this arrangement are clear," Friedman wrote in his landmark book *Capitalism and Freedom* in 1962. "It is directed specifically at the problem of poverty, and it gives help in the form most useful to the individual, namely, cash. It is general and could be substituted for the host of special measures now in effect." Friedman continued to support the idea for the rest of his life.

In the years after he wrote those words, the idea gained steam on the left as well. The focus of the civil rights movement in the late 1960s turned to economic justice, and the idea of a guaranteed income played a major role. In the final two years of his life, Martin Luther King Jr. traveled the country demanding that the government create programs to make up for decades of racial and economic injustice. King argued forcefully that all Americans should have a guaranteed income to provide them with economic stability. In 1967, he launched the Poor People's Campaign, which included a call for a guaranteed income. He planned what would perhaps have been his largest march ever on Washington for April of 1968, the month he was shot and killed.

Three days before he died, King delivered the Sunday sermon at the National Cathedral in Washington, D.C. He called for the United States to jettison its massive investment in war and to shift the country's spending to a suite of social services to shore up the income security of all Americans. "There is nothing new about poverty," he declared. "What is new is that we now have the techniques and the resources to get rid of poverty. The real question is whether we have the will."

Unlike conservative economists who envisioned "cashing in" existing poverty programs for a guaranteed income, King believed that a guaranteed income pegged to median wages and GDP growth would work best alongside an expanded set of social services. The combination of the two could abolish poverty in America for good. He foresaw a black-white coalition of laborers who would come together to overcome inevitable opposition from the wealthy and powerful, and in the year before he was felled by an assassin's bullet, he laid the groundwork for the fight.

Meanwhile, mainstream politicians and academics were studying the idea and contributing to a robust national policy debate about how it might work. In 1967, at a conference at Arden House, an estate just outside of New York City, economists and policymakers came together to discuss the relative merits of major social reform policies and left with a consensus to prioritize a guaranteed income over other similarly big ideas, like a universal child allowance. President Lyndon Johnson's Office of Economic Opportunity decided to pilot the idea in a controlled test in New Jersey, which began in August 1968. Other sites subsequently opened in Iowa, North Carolina, Seattle, Denver, and Gary, Indiana. Over the course of the following decade, more than 10,000 American families received guaranteed incomes as participants in the studies.

It was a heady time in American politics when it was possible—even fashionable—to think big on both sides of the aisle. In the years leading up to 1968, we had sent men into space for the first time, made enormous civil rights gains, and created Medicare. Eugene McCarthy, a Democratic candidate for president, embraced the idea of a guaranteed income in the presidential race in 1968. At the same time, in the center and on the right, concern grew that the nation's welfare rolls were expanding too rapidly and that the system badly needed simplification and reform. After Richard Nixon's victory in that election, his administration shocked the left and right alike when it entrusted a bipartisan group of policymakers to develop a welfare reform plan that put a guaranteed income at its center. Nixon's Family Assistance Plan proposed using a negative income tax to provide an income floor of $1,600 a year for a family of four, or around $11,000 in today's dollars. The Social Security Administration was slated to distribute the funds just as it did pension checks. Following Rhys-Williams's initial idea, Nixon's version of a guaranteed income was designed to encourage work: it phased out gradually as the incomes of families receiving it increased.

In August 1969, Nixon gave a nationally televised address—his version of a Roosevelt fireside chat—to explain his vision for welfare reform, including the guaranteed income. "The wonder of the American character is that so many have the spark and the drive to fight their way up," he said. "But for millions of others, the burdens of poverty in early life snuff out that spark."

"What I am proposing," he continued, "is that the federal government build a foundation under the income of every American family with dependent children that cannot care for itself—and wherever in America that family may live." Even though response to the speech was overwhelmingly positive, little of it was grounded in enthusiasm for a guaranteed income. The support was almost exclusively focused on welfare reform, not the promise of providing cash assistance through the negative income tax.

The story of what happened next would have outsized consequences for generations to come. Though support for the guaranteed income plan itself was thin, it passed the House of Representatives after some debate, and with bipartisan support. Once it arrived in the Senate, however, the debate grew much more fraught. Republicans grew concerned about whether the work requirements would be stringent enough and whether the bill would deliver on its promise to reduce the size of government. Democrats in turn split over the size of the benefit—many non-Southern liberals wanted it to be two or three times larger—and how to ensure no family would end up worse off under the new bill. Much of the conversation was caught up in a debate about whether people would keep working if they had an income floor. The Johnson administration's pilot programs to answer this question had begun only a few years before, and had yet to produce clear, conclusive evidence (as we will see, they later showed that people did in fact keep working). Lacking any clear way to resolve the competing interests, the bill failed in the finance committee in 1971.

According to the architect of the plan, future New York senator Daniel Patrick Moynihan, "The program was both too much and too little; too radical, too reactionary; too comprehensive, not comprehensive enough." And perhaps most importantly, it was far too complex. Even after years of debate in the House and Senate, Moynihan believed that very few legislators—the people actually voting on the measure—had any idea how much one of their constituents would receive.

After the dust settled, Moynihan predicted that future proposals would use a "flat grant system" as close to the poverty level as possible instead of a negative income tax. George McGovern proposed this in 1972 in his unsuccessful bid for the presidency. A more modest, flat benefit, clearly and simply tied to work, would have made it much more likely for the original proposal to pass.

But the failure of the Family Assistance Plan was not absolute. In 1974, Nixon signed a bill creating a guaranteed income for the elderly and disabled that still exists today: Supplementary Security Income. Nearly 9 million disabled Americans and indigent seniors currently get a guaranteed income of $735 per month from the federal government. But an even more important policy emerged from the ashes of the guaranteed income debate—the EITC that passed Congress just a few years later.

I was initially skeptical that such a wonky acronym could channel the guaranteed income's romantic values of freedom and dignity for all. The EITC sounds boring, technical, and incremental. In fact, its anodyne brand was key to its initial passage and later expansion. Ironically, the author of the program, Democratic senator Russell Long, had helped torpedo Nixon's guaranteed income plan. Long was a deep populist who made a career fighting the concentration of power and wealth in the tradition of his father, Huey Long, the populist Louisiana governor who ran the state with near-dictatorial power until his assassination. Russell Long used less blustering tactics and focused on reshaping the tax code in his role as the chair of the Senate Finance Committee. He exercised enormous power for decades in Washington, and *The Wall Street Journal* once called him the "fourth branch of government."

While Long agreed that a more active government was needed to help the poor, he took issue with the work requirements in Nixon's original proposal. That plan required people to register and prove they were looking for a job. Long preferred to create a government boost to private sector wages, creating a natural incentive to work rather than a new bureaucracy to enforce work. In 1972, Long proposed that the government provide a cash supplement of 10 percent of the first $4,000 of the annual earned income of poor families, a wage match that recipients would get once a year. The measure failed, and he reintroduced similar bills in the next two years. In 1975, he slipped the idea into a much larger tax bill, and despite its sizable cost of about $8 billion in today's dollars, President Gerald Ford signed it into law in March 1975.

Once an affordable framework was established and legislators had a sense of its effects, it became much easier to expand upon it. Every president since Ford—Democrat and Republican alike—has signed a bill to significantly increase the benefit. Legislators love this program. Most people don't know it, but the EITC, and its cousin, the child tax credit, are the most powerful tools to combat poverty that we have today. These unglorified tax credits already lift as many people out of poverty as food stamps, rent subsidies, and unemployment insurance combined. The EITC's effectiveness and popularity make it the perfect framework to use to build a modern guaranteed income.

Currently the EITC provides $70 billion in cash with no strings attached to 26 million working families and individuals. Recipients get as little as $500 or as much as $6,000 a year as a part of their tax rebate checks from the Internal Revenue Service. The calculations to determine the amount a person receives are woefully complex and depend on multiple factors: if you work, how much you earn, how old you are, how many children you have, and what state you live in. Only the rare family whose income is very stable has a sense of what they will receive year to year. But for all its mathematical complexity, the mechanics of the EITC are very simple: a check arrives once a year, and the recipient can use it however he or she likes.

The EITC's fan club is as broad and politically diverse as it is because we now actually know a lot about what happens when we provide people with cash. Dozens of studies document its positive effects. It lifts 10 million people out of poverty each year, transforming their lives:

- Kids whose families receive the earned income or child tax credit are significantly more likely to stay in school longer, and they perform better on standardized tests. Economist Raj Chetty and his colleagues have found that for every $1,000 a family receives in tax credits, students' test scores improve by 6 percent. Kids are more likely to finish high school and to enroll in college, and when they get there, they are more likely to stay there.

- In families with incomes boosted by $250 per month, children under five go on to earn 17 percent more each year than kids from families with no boost.

- For every 10 percent increase in the EITC, infant mortality rates decrease significantly. The number of babies born with low birth weights, a sign of inadequate nutrition, also decreases meaningfully.

- There is no evidence that cash benefits cause people to work less. In fact, some studies suggest that they work more. Women make more money in the years after getting a boost in their EITC than women in control groups who do not receive the boost.

- The EITC seems to slightly reduce the rates of smoking and drinking, presumably because of decreased stress levels.

Evidence of the impact of the EITC is only one part of large research base documenting the transformat of regular cash payments. The most robust data not

EITC comes from the guaranteed income experiments that were begun during the frenzy of interest in the late 1960s and continued for over a decade afterward. (Ironically, Donald Rumsfeld, as director of the Office of Economic Opportunity under Nixon, oversaw these early pilots, along with his special assistant, future vice president Dick Cheney.)

Over 10,000 families participated in these programs in six states. Families received $17,000 to $49,000 per year in today's dollars. Each location had a different pilot design, but all were focused on the question of whether people would stop working. They didn't. In 2016, a set of researchers led by Ioana Marinescu at the University of Chicago conducted a literature review of all of the analyses of the pilots to date. They found no meaningful reduction in the number of hours people worked, except for teenagers who stayed in school longer, thus delaying their workforce participation, and new mothers who reduced their working hours, presumably to take care of newborns. Families ate more nutritious food. Their children's school attendance rates went up, and grades improved. While the American studies didn't track health outcomes, a similar experiment in Canada from the same era found a nearly 10 percent decrease in hospitalizations. Cash benefits made people healthier, helped them stay in school longer, and did not encourage them to leave the labor force, confirming what studies of the existing EITC also show to be true.

I hear all the time, particularly from wealthy people, skepticism about starting with even more modest benefit sizes than the guaranteed income pilots of the 1970s provided. "How much is an extra $100 or $200 a month really going to help anybody struggling to get by?" people ask. When I channeled their skepticism to ask that question of one woman in Ohio, she locked eyes with me and answered bluntly, "Anyone asking that question has never had to choose between buying groceries and making rent." Another young student in Columbus framed it in mathematical terms, saying, "As a single person on my own, an extra $100 a month would provide me a good 20 or 30 additional meals. . . . That is something I would appreciate."

Evidence from the small guaranteed income in Alaska also shows similar results. People work just as much there as they do in the lower 48 states, but their lives are a little more financially secure. Last fall, I sat in the recreation center of a community called Mountain View in Anchorage. Its welcome sign called it the "MOST DIVERSE NEIGHBORHOOD IN AMERICA"—an eyebrow-raising claim for a neighborhood in Alaska where two-thirds of the state is white. But its residents speak nearly 100 languages, almost as many as in New York City, and they hail from every corner of the globe. In a generally white, conservative state, Mountain View is a pocket of diversity, and the people there are proud of it.

A half-dozen Alaskans had come out on a sunny fall afternoon to discuss pocketbook issues and how the Permanent Fund dividend check they get each year affects their lives. Carnard Davis, who goes by Mr. C for short, is the leader of the local Boys and Girls Club, whose teenage participants were playing after-school basketball upstairs, rumbling the ceiling over our heads. Mr. C grew up in Atlanta. He had come to Alaska on vacation seven years before and never left. "Life up here is much simpler, and as soon as I got here, I felt like I could have a second chance," he told me. "And the winter wasn't too bad."

For a single person living on a threadbare nonprofit salary like Mr. C's, the $1,400 annual check is a reliable windfall. "When you have been paying your bills for so long and then you get that pink slip saying, 'If you don't pay your $875 in rent, we are going to put you out.' . . . That's stressful," Mr. C said. "And then all of a sudden, the PFD [permanent fund dividend] comes around and helps lift that burden off of you." For anyone who doubts the power of an annual check of just over a thousand dollars to transform lives for the better, the evidence from Alaska is clear: Alaskans love it, need it, and rely on it.

Most people use the income boost to pay down existing bills like Mr. C's rent, or they save it for future emergencies or for school. A quarter say they spend it immediately. Many of Alaska's native population rely on the annual cash influx to buy heating oil for the winter. When asked, Alaskans say that the dividend does not cause them or their neighbors to work any less. Thanks in part to the dividend, Alaska has one of the lowest poverty rates in the nation, even though a meaningful portion of the state's population lives in geographically isolated areas accessible only by plane. In a ranking of states by their relative levels of income inequality, Alaska comes in dead last, 50 out of 50. It's the most equal state in the nation.

Small amounts of regular cash have an outsized power because they mitigate the ups and downs of income cycles. They reduce the feeling of living on the brink, which research unsurprisingly shows causes immense amounts of stress and poor decision-making. Historian Rutger Bergman made the provocative argument in a TED Talk that people aren't poor because they make bad decisions, but that they make bad decisions because they are poor. Why do "the poor borrow more, save less, smoke more, exercise less, drink more and eat less healthfully?" he asked. It's not because they are dim or lazy, but because they live in a mentality of scarcity. "You could compare it to a new computer that's running ten heavy programs at once," he said. "It gets slower and slower, making errors. Eventually, it freezes—not because it's a bad computer, but because it has too much to do at once. The poor have the same problem. They're not making dumb decisions because they are dumb, but because they're living in a context in which anyone would make dumb decisions."

His argument is substantiated by a deep body of psychological research that documents the effects of financial instability on the minds not just of the poor, but of the middle class as well. Harvard economist Sendhil Mullainathan and Princeton psychologist Eldar Shafir found that scarcity makes us "less insightful, less forward-thinking, less controlled." In a study they conducted in a suburban mall in New Jersey, they asked people what they would do if they had a one-time auto repair expense of $300. After thinking the question through and responding, the participants answered a set of questions from standard tests that measure general intelligence, similar to IQ tests.

The researchers then asked another group of people the same question, but added a zero to the sum, making it $3,000. Poor and well-off participants scored equally well on the intelligence test when asked what they would do if they had to deal with $300 of unexpected expenses. But the IQ level of the poorer respondents dropped by nearly 15 points when the amount increased to $3,000. Nothing had changed except the intensity of the financial stress the question elicited. "Clearly, this is not about inherent cognitive capacity," they concluded. "Just like the processor that is slowed down by too many applications, the poor here *appear* worse because some of their bandwidth is being used elsewhere." That hit in IQ points is roughly equivalent to the impact of going a full night without sleep. In other words, people who lack financial stability live each day as if they had just pulled an all-nighter, with all of the exhaustion and reduced mental and emotional capacity that come with it.

Decades of experiments and lived experience concretely show what philosophers and social movement leaders have historically believed: cash, even in small amounts, makes people smarter and enables them to live more stable, fulfilling lives. Providing a small amount of recurring income encourages people to get a job, keep their kids in school, eat better, and be healthier, likely because they're one step back from the brink and a little less stressed. We can amplify these benefits by creating a guaranteed income built on the framework of the EITC.

9

WHAT WE OWE ONE ANOTHER

We live in the richest country on Earth at its richest moment in history, even though it might not feel that way to most people. That's because nearly half the wealth in our country sits in the mansions, private planes, and bank accounts of the ultra-wealthy. Not since the Gilded Age have we lived in an era when so much wealth has been controlled by so few. The reforms of the Progressive Era, the New Deal, and the Great Society ushered in a long, stable period of shared abundance. But in the late 1970s, that pivotal moment when we changed some of the fundamental structures of our economy, the wealth share of the richest families in the United States began to grow, and the trend has not abated. Today, the top one percent of Americans controls nearly 40 percent of the wealth in our country—one and a half times more wealth than the entire bottom 90 percent own.

The debunked "trickle-down economics" of the 1980s created the most unequal economy in over a century. We now know that prosperity in America does not flow from low taxes on the ultra-wealthy, but mostly from growth in consumer spending. When middle-class families make money, they spend money, fueling economic growth and improving the lives of everyone—the poor and the wealthy alike. Studies show that when a cash-strapped person gets an extra $100, they're likely to spend it on rent, utilities, or groceries. By contrast, a wealthy person who gets the same

$100 might spend a few dollars of it, but would inevitably put most of it in the bank.

A recent study by the Roosevelt Institute, a prestigious economic think tank, shows that if we provided Americans with a guaranteed income of $500 a month, financed through a combination of taxes on the wealthy and moderate deficit spending, the American economy would grow by an additional 7 percent over the next eight years. That would mean an additional point of GDP growth each year, a significant boost to an economy that has grown at about 2 percent annually over the last several years.

Some people understandably wonder if more money in the economy would just create more inflation, diminishing the effectiveness of the policy. Economists for the most part are not so concerned that a guaranteed income would increase inflation rates, given how stubbornly low they have been for years. In fact, many believe we could use a little more inflation to lighten the load on debt holders. Even for those who are concerned, as long as a guaranteed income is financed through progressive taxation rather than government debt, the overall money supply would remain constant, reducing the likelihood of significant inflation. International studies of cash transfer programs have shown little evidence of an increase in inflation levels.

While economists and policymakers increasingly agree on the need for some kind of cash boost to working people, they continue to debate how best to do it. In a report from October 2016, the International Monetary Fund (IMF) called a basic income a "forward-looking idea" and emphasized the stability it might provide in a changing world. "In an economic environment in which job insecurity is increasing (for example, because of job market disruptions associated with technological progress), expanding available insurance mechanisms may become an important policy objective," the report said. "A [universal basic income] could provide a stable source of income to individuals and households and therefore limit the impact of income and employment shocks."

But the IMF made clear that a guaranteed income would work best in developing countries with sparse safety nets and in developed countries with spotty support systems, like the United States. (The report recommended against a guaranteed income in developed economies with strong safety nets, like much of continental Europe.) In the IMF's view, a guaranteed income works best when it is backed up and supported by other benefits that are targeted more narrowly to the poor and others in need.

Because of its historic popularity on the right, many people on both sides of the aisle hope that a guaranteed income could become an area of rare bipartisan agreement. But any real consensus between the left and right on the idea is thin at best. Libertarians see a guaranteed income as a substitute for Social Security, Medicare, Medicaid, and food stamps. They are looking to "cash in" these critical systems and replace them with a single flat payment to all Americans, rich and poor alike, of around $13,000 a year.

That kind of approach would leave millions of Americans worse off than they are today.

Republican voters strongly support Social Security, Medicare, drug treatment programs, and disability benefits, even if many of the party's leaders in Washington endeavor to cut them. We should not dismantle these programs and replace them with cash—the America we should strive for is one in which the sick have health care and the old and infirm collect retirement benefits. Many of our existing social welfare programs are not big enough, given the scope of our problems. Too few people have access to affordable childcare, paid leave, or reliable public transportation networks to get to and from a job. There are inefficiencies in some of these programs, no doubt, and we need to create a culture of honesty and transparency to highlight those failures and fix them. What we don't need to do is sweep away what works.

Trading in benefits earmarked for the poor for a benefit like a guaranteed income, which is designed to provide financial stability to the middle class and the poor alike, would be regressive, a subtle way of taking money from those who need it the most and giving it to those who need it less. By contrast, the families that would gain the most from a guaranteed income built on top of existing programs would be those who make the least, which is just as it should be.

Some of us have begun the work of providing a guaranteed income to people who need it through private philanthropy. Three years ago, the city of Stockton, California, filed for bankruptcy after the last generation's leaders had overextended the city's finances. Now led by Michael Tubbs—a new, charismatic mayor and the youngest in the nation—the city of 300,000 people is providing a small group of its citizens with a guaranteed income. (The Economic Security Project has provided seed funding for the initiative.) Community members in Stockton are determining who is eligible, how much people receive, and how long the guaranteed income will last. The intent of the demonstration is to tell the stories of what everyday Americans do when they are given a hand up through cash.

It's only a first step. In the long term, philanthropy can't meet the scale of the challenge we face. If you took all of the money that billionaires have committed through the Giving Pledge (Bill Gates and Warren Buffett's call to the wealthy to pledge to give away at least half of their wealth in their lifetimes), it would only fund a guaranteed income in America for a single year. Private philanthropy can be useful in the short term to spur experimentation and demonstrations of the idea, but to make the guaranteed income sustainable in the long term, public policy must change.

The good news is that we have more than enough money to pay for a guaranteed income to working families while strengthening our existing safety net. A boost of $500 per month to every adult living in a household that makes less than $50,000 would add an additional $290 billion a year to the federal budget, less than half of what we already spend on defense and significantly less than Social

Security or Medicare. There are many ways to finance a benefit of this magnitude. Climate activists would put a price on carbon emissions and use those funds to help poor and middle-class people while saving our planet. Others believe we might rein in the finance industry with a small tax on financial transactions and distribute that revenue to working people struggling to make ends meet. The money from either or both of these taxes could fund a guaranteed income easily. These are both good ideas that deserve more attention, but I believe the solution should be more directly tied to the problem.

The simplest and best way forward is to ask the top earners in our country, people like me who have benefited massively from the new economic forces, to pay a small part of our fortune forward. A surtax on the one percent isn't pitchforks coming for the rich or punishment for prosperity. We all benefit from a society that is more just and fair. Doctors, lawyers, and small-business owners across America all do well and may be seen as rich in their respective communities, but they are not the people who should pay. It's people like me.

First, we should adjust our tax code so that the wealthy pay the same tax rates on their investment income as hardworking Americans do on their wages. Specifically, this means ending the special tax rate on capital gains and dividends for those who make more than $250,000, raising $80 billion per year. (This is known as the "Buffett rule," after the billionaire investor Warren Buffett, who pays a lower percentage of his income in taxes than his assistant does.) Second, we should cap deductions at 28 percent for the wealthiest Americans and close tax loopholes, like the one that allows for the gains on inherited assets to be excluded from taxable income. If you inherit a mansion, you should pay the same tax as you would if that mansion had been cash. Closing these loopholes would raise $34 billion. And finally, we should raise the tax rates on income *above* $250,000 back to the historical average for much of the twentieth century—50 percent. A family making $300,000 a year would see their taxes go up only by a few thousand dollars, but a billionaire making $30 million would pay millions more each year. This change would raise $190 billion per year. These changes would pay for the entirety of the benefit without adding anything to the national debt. If economic growth accelerates as predicted, the long-term cost would be even less.

Asking the wealthy to pay their share would mean that the richest 5 million families in America would pay for a guaranteed income that would help more than 40 million families—about 90 million people—who are struggling to make ends meet.

The bumper-sticker promise would be simple: if you work to make your country better, your country will take care of you. Every American who lives in a household that makes less than $50,000 and who works in the formal economy, does caregiving at home, or who is enrolled in school would receive a guaranteed income of $500 a month. The wealthy won't get the benefit, and only the richest of the rich will pay for it.

The optimal way to structure a guaranteed income would be through an expansion and modernization of the Earned Income Tax Credit. A modern EITC would create a guaranteed income for working people and take advantage of what works in the program today, while meaningfully improving what doesn't. The money is not taxed, because technically it is a tax credit, and importantly, it does not throw people off of other government programs by counting as income from work. But currently recipients receive checks only once a year based on the size of their family, the state they live in, and their previous year's earnings. Many don't even know what the EITC is, because it comes lumped in a tax rebate check. Specifically, a new guaranteed income built on the EITC framework would be designed around these values:

Supplemental. The guaranteed income would supplement income from other sources and, for the poor, other benefits. Current EITC benefits are too low to help people cope with unreliable work and the high cost of living. A benefit of $500 per month would raise the average recipient's income by over a third. This would not be enough money for anyone to drop out of the workforce entirely, but it would be enough to make a meaningful difference in the lives of people struggling to make rent or pay for school.

Breadth. The poor have needed income support for generations, and rising costs and unreliable wages have created massive economic instability for the middle class as well. The guaranteed income would provide foundational support to both. In addition to helping more people, a broader recipient base would reduce the stigma that plagues anti-poverty programs while creating a political base for its long-term support.

Regularity. The guaranteed income would be provided monthly instead of annually to create a heartbeat of stability in the background, a reliable source of income no matter what may happen in a particular month. Over 90 percent of the participants in a pilot program that provided monthly payments of the existing annual EITC said afterward that they preferred them to lump sums.

Simplicity. Everyone who is eligible for the program would receive $500 per month by direct deposit or a debit card that regularly refills. Current EITC amounts are determined by complex formulas that make it confusing for recipients and policymakers alike, diminishing the sense of security that comes with a reliable and regular benefit and making it harder to defend the program from assaults. Targeted benefits specifically customized for each household make theoretical sense, but people want simple, predictable amounts of money they can rely on. (In order to allow for "phase out" rates, some families at the top of the income distribution, making near the $50,000 level or more, would see a customized benefit size lower than the $500.)

Visibility. Many, if not most, recipients of the EITC have little idea why they get the refund or how much it will be. They only have a vague idea of when it might arrive, depending on when they file their taxes. This lack of visibility makes it difficult for beneficiaries to recognize the benefit, talk about it, or defend it. The benefit is submerged in the tax code, which was politically necessary to get it started 40 years ago, but no longer serves its long-term interests. A flat amount transmitted by direct deposit into a family's bank account on the first of the month would ensure that recipients know their government is working to help them make ends meet. This may mean a more fraught public debate to pass the measure, but it's better to have a benefit that people can understand and defend over the long term than to hide it under the radar.

Modern definition of work. We need to expand the definition of "work" to ensure that those who are left out of formal employment but who still work—people who are meaningfully involved in childcare and eldercare or enrolled in a university—also receive the benefit. Put simply, if you made money last year, claimed a dependent on your tax return under 6 or over 70, or are enrolled in an accredited college, you would be eligible to benefit from a guaranteed income.

A significantly expanded and modernized EITC would not only help the 60 million adults receiving the money, but also the 29 million minors who live in these homes. No family would receive less money with the new benefit than they do today, and tens of millions would receive dramatically more money in a more regular and visible way.

The people who would benefit most from a guaranteed income are those who have historically been overlooked or excluded from economic development programs. Families in the lower tier of income distribution in our country are disproportionately made up of people of color. These families were also often systematically excluded from educational and financial support structures in the past. Many people of color have organized for the idea historically. As Anne Price, the president of the Insight Center, writes, "It's abundantly clear that a basic income program has much greater potential than is captured in the mainstream conversations about UBI—it holds the promise of addressing, head on, some of our most deeply entrenched racial and economic inequities." A guaranteed income targeted to households making less than $50,000 would boost the incomes of African American and Latino people in particular.

I've found that there are a number of objections to the idea of providing people with cash. The first often comes from people who have a generally charitable view of human nature, but who believe that education and skills are what matter most. Last year, during the cocktail hour before a dinner party, I spoke with a couple who were unconvinced that providing people with cash could be as important as or even more important than education. Eyebrows raised and clearly incredulous, they asked, "Don't you think it was the education you got that made your life possible?" I had sought out and benefited from a world-class education, and it had indeed worked for me—so it surely must be the most important tool to help everyone else. "Give a man a fish," goes the old proverb, "and you will feed him for a day. Teach him to fish, and you will feed him for a lifetime."

The transition to a knowledge economy has only intensified this faith. If we're creating fewer manual jobs that pay living wages, then the clear answer, it would seem, is to help people learn the skills and smarts for the high-skill, high-pay "jobs of the future." We tell ourselves that if we provide everyone with the strong foundation of a good education and make college more accessible and affordable, then anyone who has a bit of initiative will be able to enjoy a secure economic future.

In reality, knowledge sector jobs are not growing as quickly as low-paid service sector jobs, which make up about 50 percent of the workforce. Decades of investments in education at the primary, secondary, and college level have created many beautiful buildings and libraries full of books, but as we have made those investments, the sticker price for education has skyrocketed and economic mobility has decreased.

What we know from social science is that a family's financial stability can be as important as many educational programs to improve kids' performance in school. An unexpected case in point is universal pre-kindergarten, a popular policy for many on the left. Studies show that the earlier kids get into school, the better their educational outcomes are in later grades. The mayor of New York, Bill DeBlasio, made universal pre-K his signature policy in the early months of his term, and many other progressive leaders champion it.

Providing universal access to pre-K is indeed critical, but if we want to create better outcomes for kids in the long term, it would be most powerful alongside a modernized EITC to provide children's families with cash. A 2016 report from the centrist Brookings Institution compared the test scores of children whose families received cash support through the EITC to the test scores of kids who participated in universal pre-K. Its author, Grover Whitehurst, used multiple studies to measure the impact of cash supports and pre-K programs over time. He found that "family support in the form of putting more money in the pockets of low-income parents produces substantially larger gains in children's school achievement per dollar of expenditure than a year of preschool, participation in Head Start, or class size reduction in the early grades." A dollar put in the hands of a low-income family is at least doubly effective, if not more than five times as effective, as a dollar invested in pre-kindergarten.

I'm not advocating for the end of pre-K; we should not be forced to choose between educational opportunities for all kids and financial security for their families. A parent of a young child should be able to enroll her kid in preschool *and* afford monthly rent, groceries, transportation, and health care. Education for kids is important, but it should be paired with financial stability so that parents and kids can take advantage of it.

Similarly, many people think about job training as a kind of education fix for unemployed adults. Last spring, I spoke with a factory owner in Ohio who repeated what I've heard all across the country. "There are plenty of jobs here," he told me. "We just can't find anyone qualified enough to take them." Over two-thirds of manufacturing executives say they can't find enough workers with adequate tech skills.

But there is little reason to believe that federal job training programs are able to solve this problem. The federal government has run dozens of these programs for years and achieved lackluster results. In 2016, the Bureau of Labor concluded that recent investments in adult job training programs had been an utter disappointment, with the majority of participants believing the training had little or nothing to do with their eventual ability to land jobs. In fact, the more intense the government job training, the less money the recipients later earned from a job. These conclusions mirrored another evaluation, from 2012, of the Labor Department's largest job training program. It found that despite the fact that government spent $11,500 on each participant, barely a third were working in the field they had been trained in a few years later.

There is some reason to believe job training programs could improve in the future. But rather than the government orchestrating those programs, we should make it easier for people to enroll in local community colleges and vocational schools, which are more nimble and offer broader curricula than ever before. (Similarly, promising online vocational learning programs like Lynda.com and Udemy now make it possible for people to learn relevant skills for the gig economy cheaply and efficiently.)

The problem is that many people still do not have the money to be able to take advantage of the educational opportunities that would help them. You can teach a man to fish all day, but if he can't afford to buy a rod, reel, and bait, what good will it do?

Last spring, in a bar in northeastern Ohio, I sat across from a community redevelopment expert named Lisa Ramsey who had grown up outside Youngstown. The city still hasn't recovered from steel factory shutdowns in the late 1970s; in many ways, it exemplifies America's Rust Belt. As we sipped our Diet Cokes, I asked her the classic, perhaps naïve, question: "Why don't people out of work just go back to school?"

She pulled up an article on her phone and pushed it over to me. Just the week before, the local community college had announced that it was closing down—it was too expensive to keep operations going. The closest vocational school, Eastern Gateway Community College's Youngstown campus, is a 30-minute drive away. Tuition fees are $8,000 a year, and while most students receive financial aid, estimates of the average annual out-of-pocket cost are still around $1,200. And that does not include the cost of childcare, gas, or foregone wages for the time spent in school. "In a community like this where no one has savings, how are you supposed to even get started?" she responded. "It's a wonder people are able to get any education at all." Recent calls to make community colleges free would help, but people still need to recoup the monies from lost wages, childcare, and transportation to be able to take advantage of the opportunity. We have invested hundreds of billions of dollars in schools, but we have overlooked the fact that if people can't afford them, then even the best instruction won't help improve economic outcomes.

After Lisa and I finished our drinks, we joined a group that was walking around the neighborhood to talk to people who might be on their front porches or coming home from work. Some of the homes we passed were dilapidated, but many were beautiful Victorians with manicured lawns, wind chimes, and cushioned furniture on their decks. Several houses had "FOR SALE" signs in front.

One large house that looked to be several thousand square feet had a price listed on the sign: $18,000. I thought it must have been a mistake, that a zero had been dropped inadvertently. Kirk Noden, the head of the hosting local nonprofit, told me it was unfortunately not a mistake. For years, houses in these neighborhoods had been selling for less than the sum of their parts. An hour later, as we walked back to our van, I asked the question I had been thinking but had been too sheepish to ask: "If there aren't any jobs, why would anyone choose to stay here?" Kirk paused, seemingly gauging how blunt to be. "How are they supposed to leave? Where would they find the money?" The average move over state lines costs more than $5,000, an enormous sum to save if you are making the minimum wage and almost certainly hovering around the poverty line. If you can't find someone to buy your house for $18,000, you can't afford to pick up and move to the big city. Your only option would be to save enough money for the move, pack up, turn off the lights, and leave your house behind.

You might think that a job, even if it's a minimum wage gig, would give people a springboard to an education or to move to a new city with more opportunities. But over the past two years, I have heard stories of Americans who are stuck even though they're working. In 2015, *USA Today* reported the story of Cecil Euseary, a 52-year-old man who lives in Detroit and works at Burger King for 25 hours a week. His hourly wage of $8.15 earns him about $10,000 each year, nowhere near enough for him to afford an apartment of his own. He lives with his godmother and is trying to save for his own place.

Cecil is one of millions of able-bodied and diligent restaurant workers who, despite the fact that they are employed, live in poverty. Cecil's job provides him with highly variable part-time hours and no benefits, and because he is single, he doesn't meaningfully benefit from many of the government programs that target families. When we hear stories like Cecil's, many people suggest we increase the minimum wage to something like $15 per hour to help him make ends meet. They're right: a boost of that size would increase his annual pay to $19,000.

But that higher minimum wage should be paired with a guaranteed income. We need to share the cost of economic security between the businesses that employ people like Cecil and the ultra-wealthy who work for large, multinational companies. Increases in the minimum wage can put some pressure on businesses with thin margins. A guaranteed income takes from the people who can afford it and helps the people who need it. Combined with a higher minimum wage, the two would make a historic dent in poverty in the United States. With a higher minimum wage and an additional $500 per month from the guaranteed income, Cecil would join tens of millions of Americans crossing the poverty line.

Some people are skeptical that Cecil's story is all that common. They believe that people often cannot be trusted, and specifically, that poor people will just waste the money a guaranteed income would provide. One white woman in a group conversation in Detroit put it plainly: "The people that have an entitlement mentality, which is a lot of people, and they know how to work that system, will love this," she said, referring to the idea of a guaranteed income. "Who knows what they will spend it on? Booze, cigarettes, who knows what else?" She, like almost all of the other participants in the conversation that night, received some kind of government benefit like food stamps or the EITC; yet she still felt a paranoia about how an unspecified "other" might waste the money. In comments that suggested a thinly veiled racism, she believed that "people like me" would use the money well and could be trusted, but she drew a hard line when it came to lazy folks "on the dole." In other moments, these same white working-class voters shared a concern that the money would enable an opioid-addicted family member or neighbor, many of whom are also white, to buy more drugs.

But there is little evidence to suggest that cash transfers increase rates of substance abuse: tens of thousands of people who have received cash allowances and participated in studies consumed drugs and alcohol less after the transfer than before. In a World Bank review of 44 studies of drug and alcohol usage in cash transfer programs, their consumption went down in almost all of them. While it's true that addicts might spend an extra $500 on drugs, the solution to their challenge isn't to keep them in poverty—it is better substance abuse programs to help them battle their addictions.

A guaranteed income would also be a powerful antidote to homelessness. In fact, it could help prevent homelessness in the first place. A recent study examined what happens when you give a working poor person on the brink of homelessness a one-time $1,000 cash infusion. The recipients were 88 percent less likely to be homeless three months later, and 76 percent less likely after six months. "We found no evidence that this effect fades away," the author of the report, James Sullivan from the University of Notre Dame, told *Science* magazine. A single period of homelessness costs taxpayers about $20,000 in homeless shelters, policing, health care, and other costs. A small fraction of that could help cushion the periods of income instability and help people stay off the streets, while lowering the financial burden on us all.

A guaranteed income for working people would transform the lives of those in our country who need the most help. By empowering people to chase their own dreams, it would provide the equal opportunity for all that we so often talk about. It would help rebalance our economy by asking the ultra-wealthy to pay their fair share. It is the kind of big, simple idea that we should not be afraid to champion.

My father, the guaranteed income skeptic, has come around to the idea in time. We both agree that people want to work, and that if you work, you should not live in poverty. He has come to understand how unstable jobs in America are becoming and the evidence behind cash transfers. We both agree that the ultra-wealthy, not people like him, should be paying their share.

When Martin Luther King Jr. began his fight for the guaranteed income in 1967, there were 40 million Americans living in poverty. Today, fifty years later, there are still 40 million Americans living in poverty and even more lower-middle-class people who are teetering on the brink of economic collapse. We have the power to change this. A guaranteed income of $500 a month, paid for by the one percent, would lift 20 million people out of poverty and give them a fair shot at economic independence.

"The way out is through the door," goes an old Confucian proverb. Let's use it.

AFTERWORD

My husband and I are expecting our first child this year, a little boy. I worry a lot about the world he will live in and the position of privilege he will occupy. He'll grow up in Greenwich Village in Manhattan, a neighborhood that used to be full of artists and creative types, but that's increasingly difficult to afford unless you are part of the one percent. His home will be a lot larger and nicer than the one I grew up in, and his food, education, and medical care will be the best that money can buy.

But all of these advantages will be worth little if his country is fraught with instability and poverty. That will almost certainly be the case unless we change how our economy works. The natural drift of capitalism toward inequality requires a constant vigilance to make the market work for everyone, not just for the rich. That's important because most of us want a world with basic fairness, and it's also important because capitalism will break down if wealth continues to concentrate at the rate that it has in recent years. As money collects in the investment portfolios of the rich, it gets tied up in sophisticated trading maneuvers at giant hedge funds and is not usefully spent in the productive marketplaces that benefit most people.

It is possible that everything will be fine, and that our son will inherit a world where we've found a way to share our collective abundance. The scarier, more dystopian possibility is an America that looks more like the old European civilizations, in which a wealthy gentry lord over the struggling masses. The energy and entrepreneurialism of America would wither in that kind of world. We have the capacity to correct our course—and we have done so before.

Some hesitate to advocate for a guaranteed income, fearing that the idea is too big or too bold. There is little doubt that, if instituted, a guaranteed income would reset many of our expectations of what government can do for working people. It would be expensive, and it would require meaningful new taxes on the wealthiest among us. But I believe we cannot allow the defensive crouch in our current politics to prevent us from imagining and working toward a more stable and moral future. We have seen firsthand in recent years what overly cautious politics can lead to, and we've learned that we need inspirational ideas that we can build toward. When we shirk bold ideas because they're "crazy" or "outlandish," we run the risk of creating a vacuum that others fill with fearmongering or nativism.

Given the historic assaults on progressive values by Donald Trump, many of us on the left feel like we are constantly playing defense, pushing back against corruption and attempts to dismantle the safety net. This is critical work, and my husband and many friends are dedicating their lives to it. But at the same time that we play defense, we need to offensively pursue bold solutions that tap into our biggest hopes and dreams for the country we want to live in. We cannot allow our short-term political battles, no matter how important they are, to prevent us from dreaming an audacious dream and building an American economy in which everyone prospers.

The people who have benefited the most from the new economy have a particular responsibility to think boldly about economic fairness. After Facebook's IPO, my husband and I came into hundreds of millions of dollars, even though we weren't yet 30 years old. We agreed then to give away the vast majority of the money to efforts that might leave the world a more just place than the one we inherited. That has taken many paths for both of us—direct philanthropy, political activism, and unexpected byroads like the one I took to try to shore up the civic pillar of high-quality journalism. Some have been successful, and some have not. But today, when it feels like the very foundations of our democracy are at risk, we both feel the urgency of this commitment more than ever. I believe the fight for a guaranteed income, alongside the defense of the safety net, are the most urgent and important challenges we face today.

I will have failed as a parent if our son does not realize what he owes to other people and to the world around him. When he is older, I will tell him that I was part of the early stages of a great company that revolutionized how billions of people communicate, and a campaign that elected America's first African American president. I will be honest about my mistakes. I will tell him that my ambition got the best of me at times, and I will encourage him to feel no shame about embracing modest means to achieve idealistic ends. He will hear the story of where and how his grandparents grew up, how hard they worked to provide for me, and the values they passed down. I hope he will learn to appreciate their work ethic and commitment to leaving the world a better place than they found it.

And I will tell him what I know to be true in my own life: I got lucky. That the reason we are wealthy is not because of a gift of brilliance or decades of my own hard work, but because a new economy at the start of the twenty-first century created massive financial windfalls for a select few like us overnight. I will tell him that the same forces that made our fortune possible made it very difficult for the rest of America to get ahead. My hope is that I will also be able to tell him that I spent the rest of my life helping to give others a fair shot.

There is a long road and a lot of work ahead of us: there are many policy papers to write, budgets to refine, pilot projects to develop, and campaigns to fight. But at the end of that road awaits a country where every American enjoys the freedom and dignity that a stable, reliable income affords.

The moment to begin that work is now.

WHAT YOU CAN DO

Proceeds from the sale of *Fair Shot* fund the Economic Security Project, a network of researchers and activists exploring how regular cash transfers can help people adapt to the new economy. We underwrite groundbreaking economic research, support guaranteed income pilots and demonstrations, and host conferences and workshops to invite more people into the conversation about how a guaranteed income might work.

If you'd like to get more involved in the campaign, you can learn more at fairshotbook.com. Sign up for regular email updates, recruit friends and family to join the cause, or donate to the campaign.

ACKNOWLEDGMENTS

This book would never have been written without the support and guidance of a community of friends, family, and fellow activists. To my colleagues at the Economic Security Project, particularly Natalie Foster, Taylor Jo Isenberg, and Adam Ruben, thank you for your encouragement and support to see this project through. We have learned many of the lessons in this book together as a team, and I could not imagine a better group of crusaders to work with every single day.

I am in enormous debt to Gwen Hyman, for your constant coaching and endless patience as this manuscript took shape. Your reassuring presence and pointed questions have made this book what it is. Thank you for being all at once an interlocutor and guide over the past few months. Thanks to you, I will never get out of my head the question, "What work is that sentence doing for you?"

To Sarah Cannon, for the countless hours of conversation and encouragement to follow my heart and do what I want to do, not to mention your willingness to drop everything for a thorough read of the manuscript. To Genevieve Powers, who has helped me with the big stuff and the little stuff alike for eight years, through the good and the bad. Thank you for your trust and blunt transparency, and for being a rock I can always rely on.

To the trailblazers who came before me who have worked on the basic income for years, in particular, Peter Barnes and Andy Stern. Your early work and ongoing leadership have set a high bar for those of us following in your footsteps. Thank you as well to Jeremy Durant for your early look at the manuscript and research support along the way. To the California Budget and Policy Center and the Institute for Taxation and Economic Policy for indulging my frequent and impatient requests for more numbers. To Jim Levine, for believing in me and this idea when it was still in its earliest stages. To Arthur Goldwag, for your early read and careful wordsmithing. To Michael Flamini and the St. Martin's Press team for your investment in the idea and shockingly fast work to get this book out into the world.

To my parents, for teaching me the value of work and the importance of service. Thank you for trusting me so completely to tell a little of bit of your stories in this book, and for showing me that love knows no bounds.

And most importantly, to my husband, Sean. Your exacting standards and critical eye have made this book tighter and clearer than anything I could have ever done on my own. You have indulged my early mornings and late nights, patiently listened to my wandering ideas at countless dinners, sacrificed more weekends than either of us would have liked, and pushed me to think harder and be more direct. You are the intellectual and emotional companion that I never imagined I might find and now could not live without. I am so inexpressibly and deeply in your debt.

BIBLIOGRAPHY

The Ad-Hoc Committee on the Triple Revolution. "The Triple Revolution," 1964. http://scarc.library.oregonstate.edu/coll/pauling/peace/papers/1964p.7-01.html.

American Federation of Labor and Congress of Industrial Organizations. "Highest-Paid CEOs." https://aflcio.org/paywatch/highest-paid-ceos.

Andres, Tommy. "Does the Middle Class Life Cost More than It Used To?" *Marketplace,* June 9, 2016. https://www.marketplace.org/2016/06/09/economy/does-middle-class-life-cost-more-it-used.

Apple Inc. "2017 Supplier List." Apple Supplier Responsibility Program, February 2017. https://images.apple.com/supplier-responsibility/pdf/Apple-Supplier-List.pdf.

Baab-Muguira, Catherine. "Millennials Are Obsessed with Side Hustles Because They're All We've Got." *Quartz,* June 23, 2016. https://qz.com/711773/millennials-are-obsessed-with-side-hustles-because-theyre-all-weve-got/.

Badel, Alejandro, and Brian Greaney. "Exploring the Link between Drug Use and Job Status in the U.S." U.S. Federal Reserve Bank of St. Louis, July 2013. https://www.stlouisfed.org/Publications/Regional-Economist/July-2013/Exploring-the-Link-between-Drug-Use-and-Job-Status-in-the-US.

Barnes, Peter. *With Liberty and Dividends for All: How to Save Our Middle Class When Jobs Don't Pay Enough.* Berrett-Koehler Publishers (Kindle Edition), 2014.

Bastagli, Francesca, Jessica Hagen-Zanker, Luke Harman, Georgina Sturge, Valentina Barca, Tanja Schmidt, and Luca Pellerano. "Cash Transfers: What Does the Evidence Say? A Rigorous Review of Impacts and the Role of Design and Implementation Features." Shaping Policy for Development, July 2016. https://www.odi.org/publications/10505-cash

-transfers-what-does-evidence-say-rigorous-review-impacts-and-role
-design-and-implementation.

Bellisle, Dylan, and David Marzahl. "Restructuring the EITC: A Credit for
the Modern Worker." Center for Economic Progress, 2016. http://www
.economicprogress.org/sites/economicprogress.org/files/restructuring
_the_eitc_a_credit_for_the_modern_worker_0.pdf.

Bloom, Ester. "It's Not Your Imagination: Things Are More Expensive Than
They Were 10 Years Ago." CNBC, April 25, 2017. https://www.cnbc
.com/2017/04/24/things-are-more-expensive-than-they-were-10-years
-ago.html.

Bregman, Rutger. "Poverty Isn't a Lack of Character; It's a Lack of Cash." TED
Talks, 2017. https://www.ted.com/talks/rutger_bregman_poverty_isn
_t_a_lack_of_character_it_s_a_lack_of_cash/transcript?language=en.

———. *Utopia for Realists: The Case for a Universal Basic Income, Open Borders, and a 15-Hour Workweek.* Translated by Elizabeth Manton. The
Correspondent, 2016.

Bridgman, Benjamin, Andrew Dugan, Mikhael Lal, Matthew Osborne, and
Shaunda Villones. "Accounting for Household Production in the National Accounts, 1965–2010." Bureau of Economic Analysis, May 2012.
https://www.bea.gov/scb/pdf/2012/05%20May/0512_household.pdf.

Brynjolfsson, Erik, and Andrew McAfee. *The Second Machine Age: Work,
Progress, and Prosperity in a Time of Brilliant Technologies.* W. W. Nor-
ton, 2016.

Bureau of Labor Statistics. "Employment Status of the Civilian Population
by Race, Sex, and Age." Economic News Release, November 3, 2017.
https://www.bls.gov/news.release/empsit.t02.htm.

Cambridge Associates LLC. "US Private Equity Funds Return 0.2%; US
Venture Capital Funds Return 3.3% In 1Q 2016." Press Releases, September 2016. https://www.cambridgeassociates.com/press-release/us
-private-equity-funds-return-0-2-us-venture-capital-funds-return-3-3
-in-1q-2016/.

Campbell, Harry. "RSG 2017 Survey Results: Driver Earnings, Satisfaction
and Demographics." *The Rideshare Guy* (blog), January 17, 2017. http://
therideshareguy.com/rsg-2017-survey-results-driver-earnings-satisfac
tion-and-demographics/.

Card, David, Jochen Kluve and Andrea Weber. "What Works? A Meta Analysis of Recent Active Labor Market Program Evaluations." *RUHR Economic Papers,* July 2015.

Carroll, Christopher, Jiri Slacalek, Kiichi Tokuoka, and Matthew N. White.
"The Distribution of Wealth and the Marginal Propensity to Consume."
Quantitative Economics, June 3, 2017. http://www.econ2.jhu.edu/peo
ple/ccarroll/papers/cstwMPC.pdf.

Case, Anne, and Angus Deaton. "Mortality and Morbidity in the 21st Century." *Brookings Papers on Economic Activity,* Spring 2017. https://www

.brookings.edu/bpea-articles/mortality-and-morbidity-in-the-21st-cen
tury/.

———. "Rising Morbidity and Mortality in Midlife among White Non-Hispanic Americans in the 21st Century." *Proceedings of the National Academy of Sciences* 112, no. 49 (September 17, 2015). http://www.pnas.org/content/112/49/15078.

Center on Budget and Policy Priorities. "Policy Basics: The Earned Income Tax Credit," October 21, 2016. https://www.cbpp.org/research/federal-tax/policy-basics-the-earned-income-tax-credit.

Chetty, Raj, John N. Friedman, and Jonah E. Rockoff. "New Evidence on the Long Term Impacts of Tax Credits." *IRS Statistics of Income White Paper,* November 2011. https://www.irs.gov/pub/irs-soi/11rp chettyfriedmanrockoff.pdf.

Clemens, Michael. "The Millennium Villages Evaluation Debate Heats Up, Boils Over." Center for Global Development, October 21, 2011. https://www.cgdev.org/blog/millennium-villages-evaluation-debate-heats-boils-over.

Corak, Miles. "Economic Mobility." Stanford Center on Poverty and Inequality, 2016. https://inequality.stanford.edu/sites/default/files/Pathways-SOTU-2016-Economic-Mobility-3.pdf.

Cornell, C. J. "Startup Funding: Traditional Venture Funding." Rebus Community Press, 2017. https://press.rebus.community/media-innovation-and-entrepreneurship/chapter/section-3-traditional-venture-funding/.

Costello, E. Jane, Alaattin Erkanli, William Copeland, and Adrian Angold. "Association of Family Income Supplements in Adolescence with Development of Psychiatric and Substance Use Disorders in Adulthood among an American Indian Population." *Journal of the American Medical Association* 303, no. 19 (2010): 1954–60.

DeParle, Jason. "Harder for Americans to Rise From Lower Rungs." *New York Times,* January 4, 2012. http://www.nytimes.com/2012/01/05/us/harder-for-americans-to-rise-from-lower-rungs.html.

Dews, Fred. "Charts of the Week: The Jobs Gap Is Closed." Brookings Institution, August 4, 2017. https://www.brookings.edu/blog/brookings-now/2017/08/04/charts-of-the-week-the-jobs-gap-is-closed/.

Dillow, Clay, and Brooks Rainwater. "Why Free Money for Everyone Is Silicon Valley's Next Big Idea." *Fortune,* June 29, 2017. http://fortune.com/2017/06/29/universal-basic-income-free-money-silicon-valley/.

Dooley, David, Ralph Catalano, and Georjeanna Wilson. "Depression and Unemployment: Panel Findings from the Epidemiologic Catchment Area Study." *American Journal of Community Psychology* 22, no. 6 (December 1994): 745–65.

Dubner, Stephen J. "Is the World Ready for a Guaranteed Basic Income?" *Freakonomics Radio* (podcast), April 13, 2016. http://freakonomics.com/podcast/mincome/.

Dynan, Karen E., Jonathan S. Skinner, and Stephen P. Zeldes. "Do the Rich Save More?" *Journal of Political Economy* 112, no. 2 (2004): 397–444.

eMarketer. "Number of Smartphone Users Worldwide from 2014 to 2020 (in Billions)." Statista, 2017. https://www.statista.com/statistics/330695/number-of-smartphone-users-worldwide/.

Evans, David, and Anna Popova. "Do the Poor Waste Transfers on Booze and Cigarettes? No." World Bank, May 27, 2014. http://blogs.worldbank.org/impactevaluations/do-poor-waste-transfers-booze-and-cigarettes-no.

———. "Cash Transfers and Temptation Goods: A Review of Global Evidence." World Bank, Africa Region, Office of the Chief Economist, May 2014. http://documents.worldbank.org/curated/en/617631468001808739/pdf/WPS6886.pdf.

Facebook Blog. "Have a Taste . . ." Facebook, February 23, 2007. https://www.facebook.com/notes/facebook/have-a-taste/2245132130/.

Fassler, Joe. "'All Labor Has Dignity': Martin Luther King, Jr.'s Fight for Economic Justice." *The Atlantic,* February 22, 2011. https://www.theatlantic.com/entertainment/archive/2011/02/all-labor-has-dignity-martin-luther-king-jrs-fight-for-economic-justice/71423/.

Florida, Richard. *The Rise of the Creative Class, Revisited.* Hachette UK, 2014.

Flowers, Andrew. "What Would Happen if We Just Gave People Money?" *FiveThirtyEight,* April 25, 2016. http://fivethirtyeight.com/features/universal-basic-income/.

Ford, Martin. *Rise of the Robots: Technology and the Threat of a Jobless Future.* Basic Books, 2016.

Frank, Robert H., and Philip J. Cook. *The Winner-Take-All Society: Why the Few at the Top Get So Much More than the Rest of Us.* Free Press, 1995.

Freeland, Chrystia. "The Rise of the Winner-Take-All Economy." Reuters, June 20, 2013. http://www.reuters.com/article/us-column-freeland/column-the-rise-of-the-winner-take-all-economy-idUSBRE95J0WL20130620.

Friedman, Milton. *Capitalism and Freedom.* The University of Chicago Press, 1962.

Furman, Jason. "Is This Time Different? The Opportunities and Challenges of Artificial Intelligence." July 7, 2016. https://obamawhitehouse.archives.gov/sites/default/files/page/files/20160707_cea_ai_furman.pdf.

Giffi, Craig, Jennifer McNelly, Ben Dollar, Gardner Carrick, Michelle Drew, and Bharath Gangula. "The Skills Gap in U.S. Manufacturing: 2015 and Beyond." Manufacturing Institute, 2015. http://www.themanufacturinginstitute.org/~/media/827DBC76533942679A15EF7067A704CD.ashx.

GiveDirectly. "Our Financials." Accessed November 9, 2017. https://givedirectly.org/financials.

GiveWell. "The Case for the Clear Fund." GiveWell Business Plan, April 7, 2007. http://files.givewell.org/files/ClearFund/Clear%20Fund%20Detailed%20Case.pdf.

Goodman, Peter S. "After Training, Still Scrambling for Employment." *New York Times,* July 18, 2010. http://www.nytimes.com/2010/07/19/business/19training.html.

Greenstein, Robert, John Wancheck, and Chuck Marr. "Reducing Overpayments in the Earned Income Tax Credit." Center on Budget and Policy Priorities, January 11, 2017. https://www.cbpp.org/research/federal-tax/reducing-overpayments-in-the-earned-income-tax-credit.

Hacker, Jacob S., and Paul Pierson. *Winner-Take-All Politics: How Washington Made the Rich Richer—and Turned Its Back on the Middle Class.* Simon & Schuster, 2010.

Harvey, Paul. "Cash Transfers: Only 6% of Humanitarian Spending—What's the Hold up?" *The Guardian,* January 22, 2016. https://www.theguardian.com/global-development-professionals-network/2016/jan/22/cash-transfers-only-6-of-humanitarian-spending-whats-the-hold-up.

Haushofer, Johannes, and Jeremy Shapiro. "The Short-Term Impact of Unconditional Cash Transfers to the Poor: Experimental Evidence from Kenya." *Quarterly Journal of Economics* 131, no. 4 (July 2016): 1973–2042.

Hind, Dan. "Economics after Scarcity." Aljazeera.com, May 16, 2012. http://www.aljazeera.com/indepth/opinion/2012/05/201251465149622626.html.

Hipple, Steven F. "People Who Are Not in the Labor Force: Why Aren't They Working?" Bureau of Labor Statistics, December 2015. https://www.bls.gov/opub/btn/volume-4/people-who-are-not-in-the-labor-force-why-arent-they-working.htm.

Hollingsworth, Alex J., Christopher J. Ruhm, and Kosali Ilayperuma Simon. "Macroeconomic Conditions and Opioid Abuse." Working Paper no. w23192, National Bureau of Economic Research, February 27, 2017. https://ssrn.com/abstract=2924282.

Hoynes, Hilary W., Douglas L. Miller, and David Simon. "The EITC: Linking Income to Real Health Outcomes." Center for Poverty Research, University of California, Davis, 2013. https://poverty.ucdavis.edu/policy-brief/linking-eitc-income-real-health-outcomes.

———. "Income, the Earned Income Tax Credit, and Infant Health." Working Paper no. 18206, National Bureau of Economic Research, July 2012. http://www.nber.org/papers/w18206.pdf.

IGM Forum. "Robots." University of Chicago Booth School of Business, 2014. http://www.igmchicago.org/surveys/robots.

IMF Fiscal Monitor. "Tackling Inequality." International Monetary Fund, October 2017. http://www.imf.org/en/Publications/FM/Issues/2017/10/05/fiscal-monitor-october-2017.

International Rescue Committee. "The IRC's Cash Strategy, 2015–2020." In-
    fosheet. https://rescue.app.box.com/s/pawbfkvwqd9lz39ff1bh9ewlgdte
    t5aw

Karnofsky, Holden. "Should I Give out Cash in Mumbai?" GiveWell Blog,
    December 8, 2011. http://blog.givewell.org/2010/09/08/should-i-give
    -out-cash-in-mumbai/.

Katz, Lawrence F., and Alan B. Krueger. "The Rise and Nature of Alter-
    native Work Arrangements in the United States, 1995–2015 [Draft]."
    National Bureau of Economic Research, September 2016. http://data
    space.princeton.edu/jspui/bitstream/88435/dsp01zs25xb933/3/603
    .pdf.

Kaufman, Burton Ira. *The Carter Years.* Infobase Publishing, 2009.

King, Martin Luther, Jr. "Remaining Awake Through a Great Revolution."
    Speech, Washington, D.C., March 31, 1968. Accessed at King Ency-
    clopedia (Stanford University). http://kingencyclopedia.stanford.edu
    /encyclopedia/documentsentry/doc_remaining_awake_through_a
    _great_revolution.1.html.

———. *Where Do We Go from Here: Chaos or Community?* Beacon Press,
    2010.

Komaromy, Carol, Moyra Sidell, and Jeanne Katz. "Death and Dying in Resi-
    dential and Nursing Homes for Older People." *International Journal of
    Palliative Nursing* 6, no. 4 (2000): 192–200.

Lamont, Michèle. *The Dignity of Working Men: Morality and the Boundaries of
    Race, Class, and Immigration.* Harvard University Press, 2009.

Lebergott, Stanley. "Annual Estimates of Unemployment in the United
    States, 1900–1954." National Bureau of Economic Research, 1957,
    211–42. http://www.nber.org/chapters/c2644.pdf.

Lenahan, Jim, Lindsay Deutsch, Katrease Stafford, Scott Goss, and Joel
    Baird. "Hear Stories of People Living on Minimum Wage." *USA To-
    day,* October 16, 2015. https://www.usatoday.com/story/money/nation
    -now/2015/10/16/hear-stories-people-living-minimum-wage/73525
    412/.

Lewis, Michael. "Don't Eat Fortune's Cookie." Baccalaureate remarks,
    Princeton University, June 3, 2012. https://www.princeton.edu/news
    /2012/06/03/princeton-universitys-2012-baccalaureate-remarks.

Liem, Ramsay, and Joan Huser Liem. "Psychological Effects of Unemploy-
    ment on Workers and Their Families." *Journal of Social Issues,* January
    1988.

Locke, Laura. "The Future of Facebook." *Time,* July 17, 2007. phrase: http://
    content.time.com/time/business/article/0,8599,1644040,00.html.

Lowrey, Annie. "Changed Life of the Poor: Better Off, but Far Behind." *New
    York Times,* April 30, 2014. https://www.nytimes.com/2014/05/01
    /business/economy/changed-life-of-the-poor-squeak-by-and-buy-a
    -lot.html.

MacDonald, Lawrence. "Evaluating the Millennium Villages: Michael Clemens and Gabriel Demombynes." Center for Global Development, October 12, 2010. https://www.cgdev.org/blog/evaluating-millennium -villages-michael-clemens-and-gabriel-demombynes.

Manoli, Dayanand S., and Nicholas Turner. "Cash-on-Hand and College Enrollment: Evidence from Population Tax Data and Policy Nonlinearities." Working Paper no. 19836, National Bureau of Economic Research, April 2016. http://www.nber.org/papers/w19836.

Manyika, James, Jacques Bughin, Susan Lund, Jan Mischke, Kelsey Robinson, and Deepa Mahajan. "Independent Work: Choice, Necessity, and the Gig Economy." McKinsey Global Institute, October 2016. https:// www.mckinsey.com/global-themes/employment-and-growth/indepen dent-work-choice-necessity-and-the-gig-economy.

Marinescu, Ioana. "No Strings Attached: The Behavioral Effects of U.S. Unconditional Cash Transfer Programs." Roosevelt Institute, May 11, 2017. http://rooseveltinstitute.org/no-strings-attached/.

Marr, Chuck, Chye-Ching Huang, Arloc Sherman, and Brandon Debot. "EITC and Child Tax Credit Promote Work, Reduce Poverty, and Support Children's Development, Research Finds." Center on Budget and Policy Priorities, October 1, 2015. https://www.cbpp.org/research/fed eral-tax/eitc-and-child-tax-credit-promote-work-reduce-poverty-and -support-childrens?fa=view&id=3793.

Mason, J. W. "What Recovery? The Case for Continued Expansionary Policy at the Fed." Roosevelt Institute, July 25, 2017. http://rooseveltinstitute .org/what-recovery/.

Matthews, Dylan. "The 2 Most Popular Critiques of Basic Income Are Both Wrong." *Vox,* July 20, 2017. https://www.vox.com/policy-and-politics /2017/7/20/15821560/basic-income-critiques-cost-work-negative-in come-tax.

———. "Basic Income: The World's Simplest Plan to End Poverty, Explained." *Vox,* April 25, 2016. http://fivethirtyeight.com/features/uni versal-basic-income/.

———. "A New Study Debunks One of the Biggest Arguments against Basic Income." *Vox,* September 20, 2017. https://www.vox.com/policy-and -politics/2017/9/20/16256240/mexico-cash-transfer-inflation-basic -income.

———. "Study: A Universal Basic Income Would Grow the Economy." *Vox,* August 30, 2017. https://www.vox.com/policy-and-politics/2017/8/30 /16220134/universal-basic-income-roosevelt-institute-economic-growth.

Maxfield, Michelle. "The Effects of the Earned Income Tax Credit on Child Achievement and Long-Term Educational Attainment." Michigan State University Job Market Paper, November 14, 2013.

Mettler, Suzanne. *The Submerged State: How Invisible Government Policies Undermine American Democracy.* University of Chicago Press, 2011.

Michelmore, Katherine. "The Effect of Income on Educational Attainment: Evidence from State Earned Income Tax Credit Expansions." SSRN Working Paper 2356444, August 2013.

Millennium Promise, "Millennium Promise 2010 Annual Report." 2010. http://www.millenniumvillages.org/uploads/ReportPaper/MP-2010 -Annual-Report—Complete—FINAL.pdf.

Milligan, Kevin, and Mark Stabile. "Do Child Tax Benefits Affect the Well-Being of Children? Evidence from Canadian Child Benefit Expansions." *American Economic Journal: Economic Policy* 3, no. 3 (August 2011): 175–205.

Mishel, Lawrence, and Jessica Schieder. "CEOs Make 276 Times More than Typical Workers." Economic Policy Institute, August 3, 2016. http:// www.epi.org/publication/ceos-make-276-times-more-than-typical -workers/.

Moore, Antonio. "America's Financial Divide: The Racial Breakdown of U.S. Wealth in Black and White." *Huffington Post,* April 13, 2015. https://www.huffingtonpost.com/antonio-moore/americas-financial -divide_b_7013330.html.

Morduch, Jonathan, and Rachel Schneider. *The Financial Diaries: How American Families Cope in a World of Uncertainty.* Princeton University Press (Kindle Edition), 2017.

———. "The Power of Predictable Paychecks." *The Atlantic,* May 24, 2017. https://www.theatlantic.com/business/archive/2017/05/financial-dia ries-predictable-paychecks/527100/.

Moynihan, Daniel P. *The Politics of a Guaranteed Income: The Nixon Administration and the Family Assistance Plan.* Random House, 1973.

Mullainathan, Sendhil, and Eldar Shafir. *Scarcity: The New Science of Having Less and How It Defines Our Lives.* Times Books, 2013.

Munk, Nina. *The Idealist: Jeffrey Sachs and the Quest to End Poverty.* Doubleday, 2013.

National Alliance for Caregiving and AARP. "Caregiving in the U.S. 2015." July 2015. http://www.caregiving.org/caregiving2015/.

National Center for Education Statistics. "Eastern Gateway Community College." College Navigator. Accessed October 30, 2017. https://nces .ed.gov/collegenavigator/?q=Eastern+Gateway+Community+College &s=all&id=203331.

New America. "Monopoly and Inequality." Open Markets. Accessed November 9, 2017. https://www.newamerica.org/open-markets/understanding -monopoly/monopoly-and-inequality/.

Nikiforos, Michalis, Marshall Steinbaum, and Gennaro Zezza. "Modeling the Macroeconomic Effects of a Universal Basic Income." Roosevelt Institute, August 2017. http://rooseveltinstitute.org/wp-content/uploads

/2017/08/Modeling-the-Macroeconomic-Effects-of-a-Universal-Basic-Income.pdf.

Nixon, Richard. "Address to the Nation on Domestic Programs." Speech, August 8, 1969. Accessed at American Presidency Project. http://www.presidency.ucsb.edu/ws/?pid=2191.

O'Donovan, Caroline, and Jeremy Singer-Vine. "How Much Uber Drivers Actually Make Per Hour." *BuzzFeed,* June 23, 2016. https://www.buzzfeed.com/carolineodonovan/internal-uber-driver-pay-numbers.

Oransky, Ivan. "Millennium Villages Project Forced to Correct Lancet Paper on Foreign Aid as Leader Leaves Team." Retraction Watch, May 31, 2012. http://retractionwatch.com/2012/05/31/millennium-villages-project-forced-to-correct-lancet-paper-on-foreign-aid-as-leader-leaves-team/.

Our World in Data. "Price Changes in Consumer Goods and Services in the USA, 1997–2017." November 7, 2017. https://ourworldindata.org/grapher/price-changes-in-consumer-goods-and-services-in-the-usa-1997-2017.

Oxfam America and Economic Policy Institute. "Few Rewards: An Agenda to Give America's Working Poor A Raise." 2016. https://www.oxfamamerica.org/static/media/files/Few_Rewards_Report_2016_web.pdf.

Painter, Anthony, and Chris Thoung. "Creative Citizen, Creative State: The Principled and Pragmatic Case for a Universal Basic Income." *RSA,* December 2015. https://www.thersa.org/globalassets/reports/rsa_basic_income_20151216.pdf.

Pew Research Center. "Public Trust in Government, 1958-2017." May 3, 2017. http://www.people-press.org/2017/05/03/public-trust-in-government-1958-2017/).

Paul, Mark, William Darity Jr., Darrick Hamilton, and Anne E. Price. "Returning to the Promise of Full Employment: A Federal Job Guarantee in the United States." Insight Center for Community Economic Development, June 2017. https://insightcced.org/wp-content/uploads/2017/06/insight_fjg_brief_2017.pdf.

Pew Charitable Trusts. "Americans' Financial Security." Financial Security and Mobility, March 2015. http://www.pewtrusts.org/~/media/assets/2015/02/fsm-poll-results-issue-brief_artfinal_v3.pdf.

Picchi, Aimee. "Vast Number of Americans Live Paycheck to Paycheck." *CBS News,* August 24, 2017. https://www.cbsnews.com/news/americans-living-paycheck-to-paycheck/.

Piven, Frances Fox, and Richard A. Cloward. *Regulating the Poor: The Functions of Public Welfare.* Random House (Kindle Edition), 1971.

P.K. "Who Are the One Percent in the United States by Income and Net Worth?" DQYDJ, November 27, 2017. https://dqydj.com/who-are-the-one-percent-united-states/.

Pofeldt, Elaine. "Shocker: 40% of Workers Now Have 'Contingent' Jobs, Says U.S. Government." *Forbes,* May 25, 2015. https://www.forbes.com/sites/elainepofeldt/2015/05/25/shocker-40-of-workers-now-have-contingent-jobs-says-u-s-government/#3125467714be.

Poo, Ai-jen. *The Age of Dignity: Preparing for the Elder Boom in a Changing America.* New Press, 2016.

Price, Anne. "Universal Basic Income: Reclaiming Our Time for Racial Justice." *Medium,* October 31, 2017. https://medium.com/@InsightCCED/universal-basic-income-reclaiming-our-time-for-racial-justice-45de349ea06f.

Putnam, Robert. *Bowling Alone: The Collapse and Revival of American Community.* Simon & Schuster, 2001.

Rachidi, Angela. "America's Work Problem: How Addressing the Reasons People Don't Work Can Reduce Poverty." American Enterprise Institute, July 2016. http://www.aei.org/wp-content/uploads/2016/07/Americas-Work-Problem.pdf.

Ravanera, Carmina. "The Town with No Poverty: Health Effects of Guaranteed Annual Income." Population Change and Lifecourse Strategic Knowledge Cluster Population Studies Centre, Social Science Centre, University of Western Ontario, November 2012. http://sociology.uwo.ca/cluster/en/documents/Research%20Briefs/PolicyBrief10.pdf.

Rehkopf, David H., Kate W. Strully, and William H. Dow. "The Short-Term Impacts of Earned Income Tax Credit Disbursement on Health." *International Journal of Epidemiology* 43, no. 6 (December 1, 2014): 1884–94.

Reich, Robert B. *Saving Capitalism: For the Many, Not the Few.* Knopf Doubleday Publishing Group (Kindle Edition), 2016.

Rolf, David. "Why Would a Labor Leader Support a Universal Basic Income?" *Medium,* December 12, 2016. https://medium.com/economicsecproj/why-would-a-labor-leader-support-a-universal-basic-income-22d9d37e1514#.qbdr3co1b.

Saez, Emmanuel, and Gabriel Zucman. "Wealth Inequality in the United States Since 1913: Evidence from Capitalized Income Tax Data." Working Paper 20625, National Bureau of Economic Research, October 2014. http://gabriel-zucman.eu/files/SaezZucman2014.pdf.

Salary.com. "North Carolina Physician-Generalist Salaries." October 30, 2017. http://www1.salary.com/NC/Physician-Generalist-salary.html.

Salpukas, Agis. "Young Workers Disrupt Key G.M. Plant." *New York Times,* January 23, 1972. http://www.nytimes.com/1972/01/23/archives/young-workers-disrupt-key-gm-plant-young-workers-disrupt-plant-on.html?_r=0.

Santens, Scott. "Basic Income FAQ." Reddit, October 27, 2017. https://www.reddit.com/r/BasicIncome/wiki/index.

Schwartz, Nelson D. "Gap Widening as Top Workers Reap the Raises." *New York Times,* July 24, 2015. https://www.nytimes.com/2015/07/25/busi ness/economy/salary-gap-widens-as-top-workers-in-specialized-fields -reap-rewards.html.

Semuels, Alana. "Poor at 20, Poor for Life." *The Atlantic,* July 14, 2016. https://www.theatlantic.com/business/archive/2016/07/social-mobil ity-america/491240/.

Shultz, David. "A Bit of Cash Can Keep Someone Off the Streets for 2 Years or More." *Science,* August 11, 2016. http://www.sciencemag.org /news/2016/08/bit-cash-can-keep-someone-streets-2-years-or-more.

Singer, Peter. *The Life You Can Save: Acting Now to End World Poverty.* Random House (Kindle Edition), 2009.

Soergel, Andrew. "Mnuchin 'Not At All' Worried About Automation Displacing Jobs." *U.S. News,* March 24, 2017. https://www.usnews.com /news/articles/2017-03-24/steven-mnuchin-not-at-all-worried-about-au tomation-displacing-jobs.

Sommeiller, Estelle, Mark Price, and Ellis Wazeter. "Income Inequality in the U.S. by State, Metropolitan Area, and County." Economic Policy Institute, June 16, 2016. http://www.epi.org/publication/income-inequality -in-the-us/.

Spross, Jeff. "You're Hired!" *Democracy: A Journal of Ideas* no. 44 (Spring 2017). http://democracyjournal.org/magazine/44/youre-hired/.

Stern, Andy. *Raising the Floor: How a Universal Basic Income Can Renew Our Economy and Rebuild the American Dream.* PublicAffairs, 2016.

Stewart, James B. "Facebook Has 50 Minutes of Your Time Each Day. It Wants More." *New York Times,* May 5, 2016. https://www.nytimes .com/2016/05/06/business/facebook-bends-the-rules-of-audience -engagement-to-its-advantage.html.

Tabuchi, Hiroko. "Walmart to End Health Coverage for 30,000 Part-Time Workers." *New York Times,* October 7, 2014. https://www.ny times.com/2014/10/08/business/30000-lose-health-care-coverage-at -walmart.html.

Tanner, Michael. "The Pros and Cons of a Guaranteed National Income." *CATO Institute* no. 773 (May 12, 2015). https://object.cato.org/sites /cato.org/files/pubs/pdf/pa773.pdf.

Taplin, Jonathan. "Is It Time to Break Up Google?" *New York Times,* April 22, 2017. https://www.nytimes.com/2017/04/22/opinion/sunday/is-it -time-to-break-up-google.html.

Thigpen, David E. "Universal Income: What Is It, and Is It Right for the U.S.?" Roosevelt Institute, October 2016. http://rooseveltinstitute.org /wp-content/uploads/2016/10/UBI-Explainer_Designed.pdf.

U.S. Census Bureau. "Gini Index of Money Income and Equivalence-Adjusted Income: 1967 to 2014." September 16, 2015. https://www

.census.gov/library/visualizations/2015/demo/gini-index-of-money -income-and-equivalence-adjusted-income—1967.html.

———. "Household Income in the Past 12 Months (in 2016 Inflation-Adjusted Dollars)." American Community Survey 1-Year Estimates, 2016. https://factfinder.census.gov/faces/tableservices/jsf/pages/productview .xhtml?pid=ACS_16_1YR_B19001&prodType=table.

———. "People in Households-Households, by Total Money Income, Age, Race and Hispanic Origin of Householder." Current Population Survey, August 10, 2017. https://www.census.gov/data/tables/time-series /demo/income-poverty/cps-hinc/hinc-03.html.

U.S. Department of Labor. "Providing Public Workforce Services to Job Seekers: 15-Month Impact Findings on the WIA Adult and Dislocated Worker Programs." Employment & Training Administration, November 8, 2016. https://wdr.doleta.gov/research/keyword.cfm?fuse action=dsp_resultDetails&pub_id=2586&mp=y.

———. "Working Mothers Issue Brief." Women's Bureau, June 2016. https:// www.dol.gov/wb/resources/WB_WorkingMothers_508_FinalJune13 .pdf.

U.S. Federal Reserve, Division of Research and Statistics. "Changes in U.S. Family Finances from 2013 to 2016: Evidence from the Survey of Consumer Finances." *Federal Reserve Bulletin,* September 2017. https:// www.federalreserve.gov/publications/files/scf17.pdf.

Van Parijs, Philippe. "Basic Income: A Simple and Powerful Idea for the Twenty-First Century." *Politics & Society* 32, no. 1 (March 1, 2014). http://journals.sagepub.com/doi/pdf/10.1177/0032329203261095.

Van Parijs, Philippe, and Yannick Vanderborght. *Basic Income: A Radical Proposal for a Free Society and a Sane Economy.* Harvard University Press, 2017.

Velasquez-Manoff, Moises. "What Happens When the Poor Receive a Stipend?" *New York Times,* January 18, 2014. https://opinionator.blogs .nytimes.com/2014/01/18/what-happens-when-the-poor-receive-a-sti pend/?_php=true&_type=blogs&_r=2.

Vo, Lam Thuy, and Josh Zumbrun. "Just How Good (or Bad) Are All the Jobs Added to the Economy Since the Recession?" *Wall Street Journal,* May 11, 2016. https://blogs.wsj.com/economics/2016/05/11/just-how-good -or-bad-are-all-the-jobs-added-to-the-economy-since-the-recession/.

Waddell, Gordon, and A. Kim Burton. "Is Work Good for Your Health and Well-Being?" U.K. Department for Work and Pensions, January 1, 2006. https://www.gov.uk/government/publications/is-work-good-for -your-health-and-well-being.

Warren, Dorian T. "Universal Basic Income and Black Communities in the United States." 2016. https://drive.google.com/file/d/0BzQSUaxtfgvI WmRMVEhCdS1nR1hYV2RpelB4TkJVbUtSZXo4/view.

Wartzman, Rick. *The End of Loyalty: The Rise and Fall of Good Jobs in America*. PublicAffairs, 2017.

————. "Populists Want to Bring Back the Blue-Collar Golden Age. But Was It Really So Golden?" *LA Times,* June 15, 2017. http://beta.latimes.com/opinion/op-ed/la-oe-wartzman-blue-collar-age-20170615-story.html.

Weissmann, Jordan. "Why Poverty Is Still Miserable, Even If Everybody Can Own an Awesome Television." *Slate,* May 1, 2014. http://www.slate.com/blogs/moneybox/2014/05/01/why_poverty_is_still_miserable_cheap_consumer_goods_don_t_improve_your_long.html.

Weller, Chris. "Here's More Evidence That Giving People Unconditional Free Money Actually Works." *Business Insider,* July 25, 2016. http://www.businessinsider.com/what-is-basic-income-2016-7.

————. "Paying People to Climb out of Poverty Would Work If Billionaires Get Involved." *Business Insider,* November 29, 2016. http://www.businessinsider.com/poverty-cash-transfers-half-annual-foreign-aid-2016-11.

Whitehurst, Grover J. (Russ). "Family Support or School Readiness? Contrasting Models of Public Spending on Children's Early Care and Learning." Brookings Institution, April 28, 2016. https://www.brookings.edu/research/family-support-or-school-readiness-contrasting-models-of-public-spending-on-childrens-early-care-and-learning/.

Widerquist, Karl, Jose A. Noguera, Yannick Vanderborght, and Jurgen De Wispelaere, eds. *Basic Income: An Anthology of Contemporary Research.* Wiley-Blackwell, 2013.

Williams, Geoff. "The Hidden Costs of Moving." *U.S. News,* April 30, 2014. https://money.usnews.com/money/personal-finance/articles/2014/04/30/the-hidden-costs-of-moving.

World Food Programme. "Cash-Based Transfer for Delivering Food Assistance." Cash-Based Transfers Factsheet, April 2017. http://documents.wfp.org/stellent/groups/public/documents/communications/wfp284171.pdf?_ga=2.147298738.421457413.1501242755-996685541.1501242755.

Yamamori, Toru. "Christopher Pissarides, a Nobel Laureate, Argues for UBI at the World Economic Forum at Davos." Basic Income Earth Network, February 6, 2016. http://basicincome.org/news/2016/02/international-christopher-pissarides-a-nobel-economist-argues-for-ubi-at-a-debate-in-davos/.

Zuckerberg, Mark. "2017 Harvard Commencement Speech." Harvard University, May 25, 2017. https://www.facebook.com/notes/mark-zuckerberg/harvard-commencement-2017/10154853758606634/.

NOTES

INTRODUCTION

5 **income floor of $500 per month:** The Institute for Taxation and Economic Policy estimates that 18.5 million people would be lifted out of poverty with an expanded Earned Income Tax Credit (EITC) paying $500 to every adult living in a household in which total income is less than $50,000. They use the Supplemental Poverty Measure and calculate the rate using their proprietary model. This would lift 11 million more people out of poverty than the current EITC. The California Budget and Policy Center's national model comes to a similar conclusion, estimating that 19.9 million people would be lifted out of poverty with a benefit of this size. Both of their models were prepared at my request and should not be interpreted as an endorsement of the policy. See https://itep.org and http://calbudgetcenter.org/.

TWO

29 **the size and power of government consistently grew:** Income inequality also hit a record low in 1973, not an unrelated event. See U.S. Census Bureau, "Gini Index of Money Income."

29 **Government was largely perceived to be a trusted force for good**: Pew Research Center, "Public Trust in Government, 1958-2017."

30 **businesses transformed . . . the American Enterprise Institute and the Heritage Foundation into ideological juggernauts:** Jacob Hacker and Paul Pierson examine this pivotal moment in depth in their book. See Hacker and Pierson, *Winner-Take-All Politics,* 96.

32 **There are over 2 billion smartphone users in the world today:** eMarketer, "Number of Smartphone Users Worldwide."

33 **The company assembles all of these parts with labor in China and designs the devices from its headquarters in California:** Apple Inc., "2017 Supplier List."

34 **The average user spends nearly an hour a day on the platform:** Stewart, "Facebook Has 50 Minutes of Your Time Each Day."

34 **create a "social utility":** Locke, "The Future of Facebook."

34 **nearly 80 percent of all the world's social traffic is routed through Facebook's servers:** Taplin, "Is It Time to Break Up Google?"

35 **in the past 15 years, most venture capital firms have not posted much better returns than the public markets:** Cambridge Associates LLC, "US Private Equity Funds Return 0.2%."

35 **venture capitalists and independent early stage investors invested $80 billion in new companies:** Cornell, "Startup Funding."

37 **"Over recent decades, technological change, globalization and an erosion of the institutions and practices that support shared prosperity in the U.S. have put the middle class under increasing stress":** Freeland, "Rise of the Winner-Take-All Economy."

37 **Robert Frank and Philip Cook:** See Frank and Cook, *The Winner-Take-All Society.*

38 **"All of a sudden":** Lewis, "Don't Eat Fortune's Cookie."

39 **"We all know we don't succeed":** Zuckerberg, "2017 Harvard Commencement Speech."

40 **Families that have more than $10 million in assets:** P.K., "Who Are the One Percent?" There are many ways to calculate who is literally part of the top one percent. You can slice the numbers by looking at individual or household income, or by looking at the accumulated wealth of an individual or household. I use the term "one percent" broadly to describe the wealthiest Americans, households with assets of more than $10 million or incomes of $250k or higher.

40 **the average doctor in my hometown last year made $189,000:** Salary.com, "North Carolina Physician-Generalist Salaries."

40 **CEOs at S&P 500 companies who today, on average, are paid 347 times more:** American Federation of Labor and Congress of Industrial Organizations, "Highest-Paid CEOs"; Mishel and Schieder, "CEOs Make 276 Times More than Typical Workers."

40 **96 percent of the ultra-wealthy one percent are white:** Moore, "America's Financial Divide."

41 **the Waltons, all of whom inherited their wealth from the Walmart empire, now controls as much wealth as the bottom 43 percent of the country combined:** New America, "Monopoly and Inequality."

41 **The chasm between the rich and the poor has not been so wide since 1929:** Saez and Zucman, "Wealth Inequality in the United States Since 1913."

42 **Before the second half of the twentieth century, work was more likely to be at home on the farm or in a short-term stint somewhere:** Lebergott, "Annual Estimates of Unemployment in the United States, 1900–1954."

44 **Employees with 15 years of service or more received medical care for life:** Wartzman, *End of Loyalty*, 105–107.

44 **This period of stable jobs and nearly full employment was a brief historical exception:** I think this is largely because the people who write our collective narratives and histories tend to be white men, the exact demographic best served by the labor market of this period. See Wartzman, "Populists Want to Bring Back the Blue-Collar Golden Age"; and Oxfam America and Economic Policy Institute, "Few Rewards."

45 **"For workers, the American corporation used to act as a shock absorber":** Wartzman, *End of Loyalty*, 5.

46 **the numbers show it isn't just millennials doing contingent work:** Baab-Muguira, "Millennials Are Obsessed with Side Hustles."

46 **A quarter of the working-age population in the United States and Europe engage in some type of independently paid gig:** Manyika et al., "Independent Work."

46 **the number of people working in contingent jobs balloons to over 40 percent of all American workers:** Pofeldt, "Shocker: 40% of Workers Now Have 'Contingent' Jobs."

46 **of all the jobs created between 2005 and 2015, 94 percent of them were contract or temporary:** Katz and Krueger, "Rise and Nature of Alternative Work Arrangements."

46 **Many of these jobs of the new economy pay poorly:** Dews, "Charts of the Week"; Vo and Zumbrun, "Just How Good (or Bad) Are All the Jobs Added?"; Picchi, "Vast Number of Americans Live Paycheck to Paycheck."

46 **Some of these workers may get to choose when they work:** Campbell, "RSG 2017 Survey Results."

47 **Uber drivers make barely $15 an hour:** O'Donovan and Singer-Vine, "How Much Uber Drivers Actually Make Per Hour."

48 **General Motors, made twice as many cars in 2011 as it made 55 years earlier:** Hind, "Economics after Scarcity."

49 **Walmart employees working less than 30 hours a week have no benefits:** Tabuchi, "Walmart to End Health Coverage for 30,000."

49 **a factory worker who, at least in one region of Ohio, used to make $40 an hour or more:** Salpukas, "Young Workers Disrupt Key G.M. Plant."

THREE

55 **"What we're talking about here is a community that is barely surviving":** Munk, *The Idealist*, 47.

60 **she discovered that the computers had never been connected to the Internet:** Ibid., 201.

60 **researchers at the Center for Global Development at the World Bank noted that it was impossible to measure the villages' impact:** MacDonald, "Evaluating the Millennium Villages."

60 **The lead economist at the World Bank's development group called Sachs's assertions of the impact "baffling":** Clemens, "Millennium Villages Evaluation Debate Heats Up."

60 **the director of monitoring and evaluation for the Millennium Villages was forced to resign:** Oransky, "Millennium Villages Project Forced to Correct."

61 **latrines were full; garbage was piled high:** Munk, *The Idealist,* 199.

61 **"stunning transformation of 500,000 lives":** Millennium Promise, "Millennium Promise 2010 Annual Report," 46.

64 **"We scoured the Internet":** GiveWell, "Case for the Clear Fund."

65 **"Here, more than in NYC . . . I could arguably carry out a mini 'cash transfer' program":** Karnofsky, "Should I Give out Cash in Mumbai?"

66 **"By donating a relatively small amount of money":** Singer, *The Life You Can Save,* Loc. 128.

70 **digital money can be converted to traditional paper currency:** Even without other basic necessities, almost all Kenyans have a SIM card that can be inserted into any mobile phone to text, call, and transfer money to one another. If a recipient doesn't have a phone, GiveDirectly offers to sell them one by deducting it from the transfer amount.

73 **"People who received the money were happier":** Weller, "Here's More Evidence."

74 **researchers compared the responses across different groups:** Haushofer and Shapiro, "Short-Term Impact of Unconditional Cash."

75 **Most studies show no effect on the amount of time adults work:** Bastagli et al., "Cash Transfers: What Does the Evidence Say?"

75 **no evidence that cash transfers affect drinking or smoking behavior:** Evans and Popova, "Cash Transfers and Temptation Goods."

75 **"WFP takes the view that it is the people":** World Food Programme, "Cash-Based Transfer for Delivering Food Assistance." Cash also breaks the structure of donor and beneficiary by strengthening local markets. It will never make sense for a local peanut farmer to invest in her crops if aid organizations just distribute free peanut butter from America. The way to build resilient, sustainable economies is to create a market for the goods. When the participants in that market see a meaningful boost in their spending power, they are able to buy and sell goods and create stronger incentives for local entrepreneurs to invest and expand their own work.

75 **up from around 6 percent:** International Rescue Committee, "The IRC's Cash Strategy, 2015-2020."

75 **amount of cash benefits that humanitarian organizations provide is still small:** Harvey, "Cash Transfers: Only 6% of Humanitarian Spending."

76 **GiveDirectly raised more than $90 million:** GiveDirectly, "Our Financials."

FOUR

79 **The Precariat:** Precariat is a portmanteau word referring to the "precarious proletariat"—an emerging social class who struggle to get by, bouncing frequently between unemployment and underemployment. The term was made famous by British economist Guy Standing in his 2011 book of the same name, but dates back to a group of French sociologists who coined the term (*précariat*) more than 30 years ago after noting a marked increase in unstable jobs across Europe.

82 **"In terms of artificial intelligence taking American jobs":** Soergel, "Mnuchin 'Not At All' Worried."

82 **Nine out of ten economists, a University of Chicago survey found, agree:** The University of Chicago's Booth School of Business assembles a panel of expert economists who are meant to be representative of the field and polls them from time to time to "inform the public about the extent to which economists agree or disagree on important public policy issues." A 2014 poll found 88 percent of economists agreed with the statement, "Advancing automation has not historically reduced employment in the United States." Another 8 percent were unsure, and only 4 percent disagreed. See IGM Forum, "Robots."

82 **"about 95 percent of the people in the United States who want a job at a given point in time can find one":** Furman, "Is This Time Different?"

82 **A report written by prominent academics, journalists, and technologists called the "Triple Revolution":** The Ad Hoc Committee, "The Triple Revolution."

84 **financial instability and the challenges that come with weathering the ups and downs of unpredictable income are just as problematic:** Morduch and Schneider, *Financial Diaries,* 7.

85 **"Without basic economic stability":** Ibid., 4.

85 **the Pew Research Center asked more than 7,000 Americans to balance the trade-off between reliable income and more income:** Pew Charitable Trusts, "Americans' Financial Security."

86 **She cut up her ATM card:** Morduch and Schneider, "Power of Predictable Paychecks."

86 **a child born into poverty in France:** Corak, "Economic Mobility."

87 **The majority of middle-class Americans today are stuck where they are:** DeParle, "Harder for Americans to Rise From Lower Rungs."

87 **"If you're in the middle, you're stuck in the middle":** Quoted in Semuels, "Poor at 20, Poor for Life."

88 **"Middle-class life has become 30 percent more expensive":** Andres, "Does the Middle Class Life Cost More?" Not all basics have become more expensive. Specifically, if something is a manufactured good, it's probably gotten cheaper. Since the 1980s, "the real price of a midrange color television has plummeted about tenfold," not to mention the fact that they are now flat-screen media centers that connect to the Internet, as Annie Lowrey writes in the *New York Times*. "Similarly, the effective price of clothing, bicycles, small appliances, processed foods—virtually anything produced in a factory—has followed a downward trajectory." The rising cost of living in the twenty-first century is not necessarily coupled with an absence of cool stuff. See Lowrey, "Changed Life of the Poor."

88 **Housing, food, and energy costs are similarly 50 percent more expensive than they were:** Our World in Data, "Price Changes in Consumer Goods."

89 **you can't save money by sending your kids to a preschool in Beijing:** Bloom, "It's Not Your Imagination."

89 **"prices are rising on the very things that are essential for climbing out of poverty":** Weissmann, "Why Poverty Is Still Miserable."

FIVE

92 **$6,000 a year for a single person:** For people who make less than $6,000 a year, the income would be a 100 percent match of their previous year's earnings, distributed monthly.

92 **A single worker at Walmart who works 25 hour a week:** There are very important design questions about how to "phase out" the benefit to avoid creating an artificial cliff at the $50,000 mark. We don't want a lot of jobs paying $49,999 a year or to create perverse incentives for people to not go above $50,000. The organization I co-run, the Economic Security Project (more on that later), is supporting institutions to develop recommendations for how to do this most effectively in the months and years to come.

93 **A guaranteed income of this size would lift 20 million out of poverty:** The Institute for Taxation and Economic Policy and California Budget and Policy Center estimate that just shy of 20 million people would be lifted out of poverty. They calculate the rate using

the Supplemental Poverty Measure. Please see Introduction, note 1 for further detail.

93   **60 million adults with monthly checks:** U.S. Census Bureau, "Household Income in the Past 12 Months." Sixty million adults live in the 41.8 million households that, according to the census, make $50,000 or less. The approximate cost would be $360 billion. If this program is built on the Earned Income Tax Credit, which I later recommend we cash in the $70 billion spent on it each year and replace it with this benefit. The new revenue required would be $290 billion. For detailed demographic and income data, see U.S. Census Bureau, "People in Households-Households."

94   **guaranteed income at $150 per month:** As we will see in chapters 8 and 9, I recommend using the existing Earned Income Tax Credit as the framework for the guaranteed income and cash in the program. At a $500 level, this would mean virtually all current recipients would receive at least as much money as they do from today's EITC and the vast majority would receive significantly more. If the benefit size dropped to $150, however, some people could see their benefits reduced in size, clearly not my intent. It would be extremely important to protect these families and ensure that no one receives less in a future orientation of the program than they do today.

94   **"there is no guarantee that everyone will benefit":** Yamamori, "Christopher Pissarides, a Nobel Laureate."

SIX

100   **"Professionals and blue collar workers alike are putting in long hours together":** Putnam, *Bowling Alone,* 86.

103   **Work that is rewarding and meaningful . . . makes us happier, healthier, and more fulfilled:** The sociologist Michèle Lamont worked for years with men in blue collar jobs who found value and meaning in their resilience. "The collective identity of the men I talked to," she wrote, "is articulated around their struggle to 'make it through' and keep the world together in the face of economic uncertainty, physical dangers, and the general unpredictability of life." These men have created a work ethic of self-discipline that organized the focus of their days. "They don't give up, and it's largely through work and responsibility that they assert control over uncertainty. They wake up every morning, go out there in the cold, and do what they have to do to 'keep it going.'" See Lamont, *Dignity of Working Men,* 23.

103   **psychological studies also show that people who work are happier:** Wadell and Burton, "Is Work Good for Your Health and Well-Being?"

103 **it takes longer to recover from depression than it does to fall into it:** Liem and Liem, "Psychological Effects of Unemployment."

104 **Case and Deaton's work connects these "deaths of despair":** See Case and Deaton, "Rising Morbidity and Mortality in Midlife," and its 2017 follow-up, Case and Deaton, "Mortality and Morbidity in the 21st Century."

104 **Unemployed people are more prone to alcohol and drug abuse:** Waddell and Burton, "Is Work Good for Your Health and Well-Being?"

104 **Someone who is unemployed is more than twice as likely to use illegal drugs:** Badel and Greaney, "Exploring the Link"; Dooley, Catalano, and Wilson, "Depression and Unemployment."

104 **The correlation between unemployment rates and opioid abuse in particular is staggering:** Hollingsworth, Ruhm, and Simon, "Macroeconomic Conditions and Opioid Abuse."

105 **"If a man is called to be a street sweeper":** Fassler, "'All Labor Has Dignity.'"

106 **"AFDC mothers, for example, are often forced to answer questions about their sexual behavior":** Piven and Cloward, *Regulating the Poor,* Loc. 2959.

108 **labor force participation rates are higher for single black mothers:** U.S. Department of Labor, "Working Mothers Issue Brief"; Bureau of Labor Statistics, "Employment Status of the Civilian Population."

108 **"People seeking jobs would come to these local offices":** Spross, "You're Hired!"

108 **The cost would be significantly higher than a guaranteed income:** Paul et al., "Returning to the Promise of Full Employment."

109 **subsidized public-sector employment programs consistently came in last:** Card et al., "What Works?"

111 **Thirty million Americans participate in this unrecognized workforce:** Of the 49 million working-age Americans who are not doing work for pay, 16 million are enrolled in school and 13.5 million aren't working because of home responsibilities. See Hipple, "People Who Are Not in the Labor Force."

111 **nearly half of the "nonworking" poor are working to provide care for their families:** Rachidi, "America's Work Problem."

112 **We claim dependents and report the tuition that we pay:** The addition of a single check box on the 1040 Dependents section would ask if the dependent is under 6 or over 70.

112 **we can begin to recognize the contributions:** I developed the idea of a guaranteed income tied to an expanded definition of work from the work of anti-poverty scholar Anthony Atkinson. He coined the term "participation income" in 1993 along similar lines: anyone who participated in society would receive a basic income. Questions about how to

"verify" participation have plagued his proposal for years. My proposal, as outlined in the next chapter, ties the guaranteed income to work activities like wage labor, childcare, or study, all of which are reported on annual tax returns and verified by existing audit procedures. Perhaps after establishing a guaranteed income tied to an expanded definition of work, the next step might be a broader "participation income" as Atkinson outlined.

112 **Our country's fastest-growing demographic is people over age 85:** Poo, *Age of Dignity,* 3.

112 **majority of people who end up in nursing homes die within two years:** Komaromy, Sidell, and Katz, "Death and Dying"; Poo, *Age of Dignity,* 31.

113 **people who take on care and housing responsibilities pay a steep personal cost:** National Alliance for Caregiving and AARP, "Caregiving in the U.S. 2015."

113 **"Seventy percent of caregivers report making changes":** Poo, *Age of Dignity,* 64.

113 **"Often they do this without support":** Ibid., 27.

114 **over \$4 trillion of economic activity is going unrecognized:** Bridgman et al., "Accounting for Household Production."

SEVEN

118 **Facebook's growing popularity:** Facebook Blog, "Have a Taste . . ."

132 **"The dignity of the individual":** King, *Where Do We Go from Here,* 173.

137 **That plan was defeated:** Barnes, *With Liberty and Dividends for All,* Loc. 70.

EIGHT

143 **"The advantages of this arrangement are clear":** Friedman, *Capitalism and Freedom,* 192.

144 **The focus of the civil rights movement in the late 1960s turned to economic justice:** The Black Panther Party began to agitate for the idea of a guaranteed income and incorporated it into its Ten-Point program, the "Bill of Rights" of the party.

144 **"There is nothing new about poverty":** King, "Remaining Awake Through a Great Revolution."

146 **"The wonder of the American character":** Nixon, "Address to the Nation on Domestic Programs."

147 **"The program was both too much and too little":** Moynihan, *Politics of a Guaranteed Income,* 506.

148 **Moynihan predicted that future proposals:** Ibid., 551.

149 *The Wall Street Journal* **once called him the "fourth branch of government":** Kaufman, *Carter Years,* 293.

150 **unglorified tax credits already lift as many people out of poverty:** Center on Budget and Policy Priorities, "Policy Basics."

150 **the mechanics of the EITC are very simple:** Ibid.

150 **Dozens of studies document:** Many of these studies have been conducted on families receiving the EITC, and others have been done on similar unconditional cash transfer programs.

151 **Kids are more likely to finish high school and to enroll in college:** Maxfield, "Effects of the Earned Income Tax Credit"; Manoli and Turner, "Cash-on-Hand"; Michelmore, "Effect of Income on Educational Attainment"; Milligan and Stabile, "Do Child Tax Benefits Affect the Well-Being of Children?"; Chetty, Friedman, and Rockoff, "New Evidence."

151 **children under five go on to earn 17 percent more each year:** Marr et al., "EITC and Child Tax Credit."

151 **number of babies born with low birth weights . . . also decreases meaningfully:** Ravanera, "Town with No Poverty"; Costello et al., "Association of Family Income"; Hoynes, Miller, and Simon, "Income, the Earned Income Tax Credit"; Hoynes, Miller, and Simon, "EITC."

151 **Women make more money in the years after getting a boost in their EITC:** Marr et al., "EITC and Child Tax Credit."

151 **The EITC seems to slightly reduce the rates of smoking and drinking:** Rehkopf, Strully, and Dow, "Short-Term Impacts."

152 **the American studies didn't track health outcomes:** Marinescu, "No Strings Attached."

154 **the dividend does not cause them or their neighbors to work any less:** Ibid.

155 **Alaska comes in dead last:** Sommeiller, Price, and Wazeter, "Income Inequality in the U.S."

155 **"You could compare it to a new computer":** Bregman, "Poverty Isn't a Lack of Character."

155 **scarcity makes us "less insightful":** Mullainathan and Shafir, *Scarcity,* 13.

156 **"Clearly, this is not about inherent cognitive capacity":** Ibid., 52.

NINE

160 **the wealth share of the richest families in the United States began to grow:** Saez and Zucman, "Wealth Inequality in the United States Since 1913."

160 **the top one percent of Americans controls nearly 40 percent of the wealth in our country:** U.S. Federal Reserve, Division of Research and Statistics, "Changes in U.S. Family Finances."

160 **a wealthy person who gets the same $100:** Dynan, Skinner, and Zeldes, "Do the Rich Save More?"; Carroll et al., "Distribution of Wealth." Economist J. W. Mason makes a robust case that we need more consumer spending to increase productivity and boost the economy. See Mason, "What Recovery?"

161 **A recent study by the Roosevelt Institute:** Nikiforos, Steinbaum, and Zezza, "Modeling the Macroeconomic Effects."

161 **International studies of cash transfer programs have shown little evidence:** Matthews, "New Study Debunks."

162 **"In an economic environment":** IMF Fiscal Monitor, "Tackling Inequality."

164 **boost of $500 per month to every adult:** The boost would work as previously described as an expanded EITC, adding $290 billion to the existing $70 billion of costs for a total of $360 billion. U.S. Census data shows that 60 million adults between ages 18 and 65 live in 42 million households with total incomes of less than $50,000 per year. These numbers are purposefully high; they assume that all adults in households with total incomes under $50,000 work in some way and all take the benefit. See https://www.census.gov/data.html.

168 **90 percent of the participants in a pilot program:** Bellisle and Marzahl, "Restructuring the EITC."

168 **people want simple, predictable amounts of money they can rely on:** The complexity of the current benefit also gives its critics the authority to claim a high "fraud rate" of 25 percent. In reality, this "fraud" is more often than not the result of complexity in knowing who qualifies for the benefit and when, as the IRS itself acknowledges. As the Center on Budget and Policy Priorities writes on its website, "The EITC is one of the most complex elements of the tax code that individual taxpayers face. The IRS instructions for the credit are nearly twice as long as the 13 pages of instructions for the Alternative Minimum Tax, which is widely viewed as difficult. The EITC's complexity is in significant part because of efforts by Congress to target the credit to families in need and thereby limit its budgetary cost. EITC overpayments often result from the interaction between the complexity of the EITC rules and the complexity of families' lives. The Treasury Department has estimated that 70 percent of EITC improper payments stem from issues related to the EITC's residency and relationship requirements, which are complicated; filing status issues, which can arise when married couples file (often following a separation) as singles or heads of households; and other issues related to who can claim a child in non-traditional family

arrangements." Greenstein, Wancheck, and Marr. "Reducing Overpayments in the Earned Income Tax Credit."

169 **submerged in the tax code:** The Cornell professor Suzanne Mettler examines the effect of hiding a variety of progressive policies in the tax code and thus obscuring them from the view of everyday people. When policies are invisible and confusing, beneficiaries are less likely to understand and defend them. They breed a cynicism that government does little and doesn't work for everyday people. See Mettler, *The Submerged State*.

170 **significantly expanded and modernized EITC would not only help the 60 million adults:** U.S. Census Bureau, "People in Households-Households."

170 **tens of millions would receive dramatically more money:** Single people with two or more children can currently receive as much as $6,269 per year depending on their earnings. For the small number of families who receive this amount, the IRS would send an annual check for the $269 to ensure that they would not inadvertently see a cut to their benefits because of the new policy. See Center on Budget and Policy Priorities, "Policy Basics." A related policy that should like be expanded at the same time is the child tax credit, which, if modified, could private a recurring, monthly cash allowance to adults based on the number of children they have.

170 **"It's abundantly clear that a basic income program has much greater potential":** Price, "Universal Basic Income."

171 **knowledge sector jobs are not growing as quickly:** Florida, *Rise of the Creative Class*, 44–49.

172 **"family support in the form of putting more money in the pockets of low-income parents":** Whitehurst, "Family Support or School Readiness?"

173 **two-thirds of manufacturing executives say they can't find enough workers with adequate tech skills:** Giffi et al., "Skills Gap in U.S. Manufacturing."

173 **the more intense the government job training:** U.S. Department of Labor, "Providing Public Workforce Services."

173 **barely a third were working in the field they had been trained in:** Job training programs have worked when industries have been willing to get their hands dirty and involve themselves in the process. In one example from 2002, the California Association of Health Facilities received several million dollars of state funding to train 2,000 new certified nursing assistants, and more than 90 percent of them landed jobs. But the results of similar programs have at other times come up short. A Michigan No Worker Left Behind program developed with the same philosophy focused on high-impact training in industries like energy

storage and aircraft mechanics, and 41 percent of the 2009 graduates from this program were still looking for work a year later. See Goodman, "After Training."

174 **There is some reason to believe job training programs could improve:** Just as with pre-K, I have no ideological objection to job training programs, and there is reason to believe that programs could improve in future years. The Obama administration worked to narrow the gap between the skills learned in training and the abilities needed to fill real vacancies. The federal approach in recent years has turned toward training in partnership with industry associations, backed up by certifications from accredited academic institutions at the end. There are good reasons to believe this could be successful, but reliable data thus far is hard to come by.

174 **Tuition fees are $8,000 a year:** National Center for Education Statistics, "Eastern Gateway Community College."

176 **The average move over state lines costs more than $5,000:** Williams, "Hidden Costs of Moving."

176 *USA Today* **reported the story of Cecil Euseary:** Lenahan et al., "Stories of People Living on Minimum Wage."

178 **there is little evidence to suggest that cash transfers increase rates of substance abuse:** Velasquez-Manoff, "What Happens When the Poor Receive a Stipend?"

178 **a World Bank review of 44 studies of drug and alcohol usage:** Evans and Popova, "Do the Poor Waste Transfers?"

179 **"We found no evidence that this effect fades away":** Shultz, "Bit of Cash."